SP 800-32

Introduction to Public Key Technology and the Federal PKI Infrastructure

D. Richard Kuhn
Vincent C. Hu
W. Timothy Polk
Shu-Jen Chang

26 February 2001

National Institute of Standards and Technology

FORWARD/COMMENTARY

The National Institute of Standards and Technology (NIST) is a measurement standards laboratory, and a non-regulatory agency of the United States Department of Commerce. Its mission is to promote innovation and industrial competitiveness. Founded in 1901, as the National Bureau of Standards, NIST was formed with the mandate to provide standard weights and measures, and to serve as the national physical laboratory for the United States. With a world-class measurement and testing laboratory encompassing a wide range of areas of computer science, mathematics, statistics, and systems engineering, NIST's cybersecurity program supports its overall mission to promote U.S. innovation and industrial competitiveness by advancing measurement science, standards, and related technology through research and development in ways that enhance economic security and improve our quality of life.

The need for cybersecurity standards and best practices that address interoperability, usability and privacy has been shown to be critical for the nation. NIST's cybersecurity programs seek to enable greater development and application of practical, innovative security technologies and methodologies that enhance the country's ability to address current and future computer and information security challenges.

The cybersecurity publications produced by NIST cover a wide range of cybersecurity concepts that are carefully designed to work together to produce a holistic approach to cybersecurity primarily for government agencies and constitute the best practices used by industry. This holistic strategy to cybersecurity covers the gamut of security subjects from development of secure encryption standards for communication and storage of information while at rest to how best to recover from a cyber-attack.

Why buy a book you can download for free?

Some are available only in electronic media. Some online docs are missing pages or barely legible.

We at 4th Watch Books are former government employees, so we know how government employees actually use the standards. When a new standard is released, an engineer prints it out, punches holes and puts it in a 3-ring binder. While this is not a big deal for a 5 or 10-page document, many NIST documents are over 100 pages and printing a large document is a time-consuming effort. So, an engineer that's paid $75 an hour is spending hours simply printing out the tools needed to do the job. That's time that could be better spent doing engineering. We publish these documents so engineers can focus on what they were hired to do – engineering. It's much more cost-effective to just order the latest version from Amazon.com

If there is a standard you would like published, let us know. Our web site is Cybah.webplus.net

Please see the Cybersecurity Standards list at the end of this book.

CyberSecurity Standards Library™

Get a Complete Library of Over 300 Cybersecurity Standards on 1 Convenient DVD!

The **4th Watch CyberSecurity Standards Library** is a DVD disc that puts over 300 current and archived cybersecurity standards from NIST, DOD, DHS, CNSS and NERC at your fingertips! Many of these cybersecurity standards are hard to find and we included the current version and a previous version for many of them. The DVD includes four books written by Luis Ayala: **The Cyber Dictionary, Cybersecurity Standards, Cyber-Security Glossary of Building Hacks and Cyber-Attacks**, and **Cyber-Physical Attack Defenses: Preventing Damage to Buildings and Utilities**.

- ✓ DVD includes many Hard-to-find Cybersecurity Standards - some still in Draft.
- ✓ Docs are organized by source and listed numerically so each standard is easy to locate.
- ✓ The listing of standards on the DVD includes an abstract of the subject, and date issued.
- ✓ PDF format for use on PC, Mac, eReaders, or tablets.
- ✓ No need for WiFi / Internet.
- ✓ Save countless hours of searching and downloading.
- ✓ Carry in a briefcase - terrific for travel.

4th Watch Publishing is releasing the CyberSecurity Standards Library DVD to make it easier for you to access the tools you need to ensure the security of your computer networks and SCADA systems. We also publish many of these standards on demand so you don't need to waste valuable time searching for the latest version of a standard, printing hundreds of pages and punching holes so they can go in a three-ring binder. **Order on Amazon.com**

The DVD works on PC and Mac with the standards in PDF format. To view the CyberSecurity Standards Library on the DVD, a computer with a DVD drive is required. The most current version of your internet browser, at least 2GB of RAM, and current version of Adobe Reader is recommended. (Compatible browsers include Internet Explorer 8+, Mozilla Firefox 4+, Apple Safari 5+, Google Chrome 15+)

Portions of this document have been abstracted from other U.S. Government publications, including: "Minimum Interoperability Specification for PKI Components (MISPC), Version 1" NIST SP 800-15, January 1998; "Certification Authority Systems", OCC 99-20, Office of the Comptroller of the Currency, May 4, 1999; "Guideline for Implementing Cryptography in the Federal Government", NIST SP800-21, November 1999; Advances and Remaining Challenges to Adoption of Public Key Infrastructure Technology, U.S. General Accounting Office, GAO-01-277, February, 2001.
Additional portions were used with permission from "Planning for PKI: Best practices for PKI Deployment", R. Housley and T. Polk, Wiley & Sons, 2001. John Wack contributed material on PKI architectures.

1	**INTRODUCTION**	5
	1.1 GOALS	5
	1.2 MOTIVATION	5
	1.3 OVERVIEW	6
2	**BACKGROUND**	7
	2.1 SECURITY SERVICES	7
	2.2 NON-CRYPTOGRAPHIC SECURITY MECHANISMS	7
	2.2.1 *Parity Bits and Cyclic Redundancy Checks*	7
	2.2.2 *Digitized Signatures*	8
	2.2.3 *PINs and Passwords*	8
	2.2.4 *Biometrics*	8
	2.2.5 *Summary - Non-Cryptographic Security Mechanisms*	9
	2.3 CRYPTOGRAPHIC SECURITY MECHANISMS	9
	2.3.1 *Symmetric Key*	9
	2.3.2 *Secure Hash*	10
	2.3.3 *Asymmetric (public key) Cryptography*	11
	2.3.4 *Summary – Cryptographic Mechanisms*	12
	2.4 SECURITY INFRASTRUCTURES	13
3	**PUBLIC KEY INFRASTRUCTURES**	15
	3.1 PKI COMPONENTS	16
	3.1.1 *Certification Authorities*	17
	3.1.2 *Registration Authorities*	17
	3.1.3 *PKI Repositories*	18
	3.1.4 *Archives*	18
	3.1.5 *PKI users*	18
	3.2 PKI ARCHITECTURES	18
	3.2.1 *Enterprise PKI Architectures*	19
	3.2.2 *Bridge PKI Architecture*	20
	3.2.3 *Physical Architecture*	20
	3.3 PKI DATA STRUCTURES	22
	3.3.1 *X.509 Public Key Certificates*	22
	3.3.2 *Certificate Revocation Lists (CRLs)*	24
	3.3.3 *Attribute Certificates*	26
	3.4 ADDITIONAL PKI SERVICES	26
	3.5 CASE STUDY	27
4	**ISSUES AND RISKS IN CA SYSTEM OPERATION**	29
	4.1 VERIFYING IDENTITY	29
	4.2 CERTIFICATE CONTENT	29
	4.3 CERTIFICATE CREATION, DISTRIBUTION, AND ACCEPTANCE	30
	4.4 MANAGING DIGITAL CERTIFICATES	30
	4.4.1 *Customer Disclosures*	30
	4.4.2 *Subscriber Service and Support*	31
	4.4.3 *Suspending and Revoking Certificates*	31
	4.4.4 *Processing Relying Party Requests*	32
	4.4.5 *Certificate Revocation*	32
5	**THE FEDERAL PKI**	33
	5.1 FEDERAL PKI ARCHITECTURE	33
	5.2 FEDERAL CERTIFICATE PROFILE(S)	35
	5.3 FEDERAL CRL PROFILE(S)	37
6	**DEPLOYING AN AGENCY PKI**	38

6.1   ANALYZE DATA AND APPLICATIONS FOR YOUR ORGANIZATION 38

6.2   COLLECT SAMPLE POLICIES AND BASE STANDARDS 39

6.3   DRAFT CERTIFICATE POLICY(S) 39

    6.3.1   *Certificate Policies* *40*

    6.3.2   *Computer Security Objects Registry* *41*

    6.3.3   *Establishing Policy Mappings and Constraints* *41*

    6.3.4   *Local certificate and CRL profile(s)* *41*

6.4   SELECT PKI PRODUCT OR SERVICE PROVIDER 42

6.5   DEVELOP CPS (CERTIFICATION PRACTICE STATEMENT) 42

6.6   DO A PILOT 43

6.7   APPLY FOR CROSS CERTIFICATION WITH THE FBCA 43

7   SUMMARY AND CONCLUSIONS **44**

8   ACRONYMS AND ABBREVIATIONS **45**

9   GLOSSARY **46**

10   SELECTED BIBLIOGRAPHY **53**

1 INTRODUCTION

Public Key Infrastructures (PKIs) can speed up and simplify delivery of products and services by providing electronic approaches to processes that historically have been paper based. These electronic solutions depend on data integrity and authenticity. Both can be accomplished by binding a unique digital signature to an individual and ensuring that the digital signature cannot be forged. The individual can then digitally sign data and the recipient can verify the originator of the data and that the data has not been modified without the originator's knowledge. In addition, the PKI can provide encryption capabilities to ensure privacy.

As with all aspects of information technology, introducing a PKI into an organization requires careful planning and a thorough understanding of its relationship to other automated systems. This document provides a brief overview of issues related to the emerging Federal public key infrastructure, and its implementation within government agencies. It also reviews the risks and benefits of various PKI components, and some of the tradeoffs that are possible in the implementation and operation of PKIs within the Federal government.

1.1 GOALS

This publication was developed to assist agency decision-makers in determining if a PKI is appropriate for their agency, and how PKI services can be deployed most effectively within a Federal agency. It is intended to provide an overview of PKI functions and their applications. Additional documentation will be required to fully analyze the costs and benefits of PKI systems for agency use, and to develop plans for their implementation. This document provides a starting point and references to more comprehensive publications.

1.2 MOTIVATION

Practically every organization is looking to the Internet to deliver services, sell products, and cut costs. Federal agencies are under additional pressure to deliver Internet-based services to satisfy legislative and regulatory requirements. Two of the laws that motivate federal agencies to offer services electronically are the Government Paperwork Elimination Act (GPEA) [NARA 00] and the Health Insurance Portability and Accountability Act (HIPAA) [HCFA 01].

The Government Paperwork Elimination Act requires Federal agencies to offer services electronically. GPEA requires Federal agencies, by October 21, 2003, to provide an option to submit information or perform transactions electronically and to maintain records electronically. The law specifically establishes the legal standing of electronic records and their related electronic signatures.

Agencies are required to use electronic authentication methods to verify the identity of the sender and the integrity of electronic content. GPEA defines electronic signature as any method of signing an electronic message that identifies and authenticates the person who is the source of the message and indicates their approval of the contents.

The Health Insurance Portability and Accountability Act was passed in 1996. One part of this legislation was designed to improve efficiency through the use of uniform electronic data exchange mechanisms for health information. To achieve this, HIPAA required electronic processing and transmission of administrative and financial health care information. To address privacy and security concerns, HIPAA also mandates security and privacy standards to protect this health information.

Neither GPEA nor HIPAA mandates the use of specific technologies. Instead, they establish requirements to deliver services or transmit information while protecting the privacy and integrity of the citizen. However, the broad range of requirements established in these laws promotes the use of a comprehensive security infrastructure, such as PKI. Digital signatures and PKI offer a very strong mechanism to implement these requirements.

1.3 OVERVIEW

This document is divided into six sections. This section describes the motivations and contents of the document. Section 2, Background, describes the security services, mechanisms that have been used historically, and the rationale for supporting these services through a public key infrastructure. This section also explains why traditional security mechanisms may need to be supplemented with PKI functions for many applications. Section 3, Public Key Infrastructures, describes the technology on which PKI is based, and shows how public key systems provide security. Section 4 is devoted to operation of a key PKI component, the certification authority. In this section, some of the risk/benefit tradeoffs in operating an agency PKI system are described. Section 5 introduces the Federal PKI (FPKI) and some of the considerations for agencies that plan to connect with the FPKI. Finally, Section 6 provides a brief overview of the procedures required to set up a PKI within a Federal agency.

2 BACKGROUND

This section is intended to describe the security services that may be achieved, and provide a comparison for the various techniques that may be used.

2.1 SECURITY SERVICES

There are four basic security services: integrity, confidentiality, identification and authentication, and non-repudiation. This section describes the four services and why they may be necessary in a particular application.

Data integrity services address the unauthorized or accidental modification of data. This includes data insertion, deletion, and modification. To ensure data integrity, a system must be able to detect *unauthorized* data modification. The goal is for the receiver of the data to verify that the data has not been altered.

Confidentiality services restrict access to the content of sensitive data to only those individuals who are authorized to view the data. Confidentiality measures prevent the *unauthorized* disclosure of information to unauthorized individuals or processes.

Identification and authentication services establish the validity of a transmission, message, and its originator. The goal is for the receiver of the data to determine its origin.

Non-repudiation services prevent an individual from denying that previous actions had been performed. The goal is to ensure that the recipient of the data is assured of the sender's identity.

2.2 NON-CRYPTOGRAPHIC SECURITY MECHANISMS

Some of the security services described above can be achieved without the use of cryptography. Where illustrations may be useful, we will use Alice, Bob, and Charlie. Alice and Bob want to communicate in a secure manner. Charlie would like to interfere with the security services that Alice and Bob would like to obtain.

2.2.1 Parity Bits and Cyclic Redundancy Checks

The simplest security mechanisms were designed to ensure the integrity of data transmitted between devices (e.g., computers and terminals). When devices communicate over a noisy channel, such as a phone line, there was a possibility that data might be altered. To guard against this, systems would transmit an extra bit, the parity bit, for each byte of data. The value of the extra bit was chosen to ensure that the number of 1s in the nine bits were odd (odd parity) or even (even parity). If the parity was wrong, data had been altered, and should be rejected. This mechanism is frequently used with modem connections.

Parity bits are a relatively expensive form of integrity protection. They increase the size of the message by at least 12.5%. Worse, they may not detect multiple errors in the same byte. While this mechanism can be extended to detect such errors by using additional parity bits, the cost is increased yet again.

Cyclic redundancy checks, or CRCs, perform the same function for larger streams of data with less overhead. CRCs are calculated by the sender using a mathematical function applied to the data to be transmitted to create a fixed size output. The CRC is appended to the transmitted data.   The receiver calculates the CRC from the data stream and matches it against the CRC provided by the sender. If the two match, the data has not changed accidentally. This technique is commonly used in network protocols, such as Ethernet.

Parity bits and CRCs protect against accidental modification of data, but do not protect against an attacker. If Alice sends a message to Bob, he can use these techniques as protection against a noisy channel, but a knowledgeable attacker could replace or modify the message without detection.

2.2.2 Digitized Signatures

In the paper world, the traditional mechanism for non-repudiation is the handwritten signature. This signature indicates that the signer has written, approved, or acknowledged the contents of the paper document. A digitized signature is sometimes used as a substitute for written signatures when applications are computerized.

A digitized signature is created by scanning in a handwritten signature. When someone wishes to sign an electronic document, they simply insert the image of their signature where appropriate. When the receiver views an electronic document or message, they immediately recognize the meaning of the digitized signature.

Digitized signatures are one of the easiest mechanisms to use. If Bob knows Alice's signature, he will recognize it right away. However, they are also one of the easiest to subvert. Charlie can easily cut Alice's digitized signature from one document and insert it into another. Digitized signatures should not be relied upon for any security services. Digitized signatures are generally used in conjunction with a stronger mechanism to add usability.

2.2.3 PINs and Passwords

The traditional method for authenticating users has been to provide them with a personal identification number or secret password, which they must use when requesting access to a particular system. Password systems can be effective if managed properly, but they seldom are. Authentication that relies solely on passwords has often failed to provide adequate protection for computer systems for a number of reasons. If users are allowed to make up their own passwords, they tend to choose ones that are easy to remember and therefore easy to guess. If passwords are generated from a random combination of characters, users often write them down because they are difficult to remember. Where password-only authentication is not adequate for an application, it is often used in combination with other security mechanisms.

PINs and passwords do not provide non-repudiation, confidentiality, or integrity. If Alice wishes to authenticate to Bob using a password, Bob must also know it. Since both Alice and Bob know the password, it is difficult to prove which of them performed a particular operation.

2.2.4 Biometrics

Biometric authentication relies on a unique physical characteristic to verify the identity of system users. Common biometric identifiers include fingerprints, written signatures, voice patterns, typing patterns, retinal scans, and hand geometry. The unique pattern that identifies a user is formed during an enrollment process, producing a template for that user.

When a user wishes to authenticate to the system, a physical measurement is made to obtain a current biometric pattern for the user. This pattern can then be compared against the enrollment template in order to verify the user's identity. Biometric authentication devices tend to cost more than password or token-based systems, because the hardware required to capture and analyze biometric patterns is more complicated. However, biometrics provide a very high level of security because the authentication is directly related to a unique physical characteristic of the user which is more difficult to counterfeit. Recent technological advances have also helped to reduce the cost of biometric authentication systems.

2.2.5 Summary - Non-Cryptographic Security Mechanisms

Non-cryptographic mechanisms may be used to authenticate the identity of a user or verify the integrity of data that has been transmitted over a communications line. None of these mechanisms provide confidentiality or non-repudiation. In general, cryptographic security mechanisms are required to achieve confidentiality or non-repudiation.

Mechanism	Data integrity	Confidentiality	Identification and authentication	Non-repudiation
Parity bits and CRCs	Yes	No	No	No
Digitized signatures	No	No	No	No
PINs and passwords	No	No	Yes	No
Biometrics	No	No	Yes	No

2.3 CRYPTOGRAPHIC SECURITY MECHANISMS

Cryptography is a branch of applied mathematics concerned with transformations of data for security. In cryptography, a sender transforms unprotected information (plaintext) into coded text (ciphertext). A receiver uses cryptography to either (a) transform the ciphertext back into plaintext, (b) verify the sender's identity, (c) verify the data's integrity, or some combination.

In many cases, the sender and receiver will use *keys* as an additional input to the cryptographic algorithm. With some algorithms, it is critical that the keys remain a secret. If Charlie is able to obtain secret keys, he can pretend to be Alice or Bob, or read their private messages. One of the principal problems associated with cryptography is getting secret keys to authorized users without disclosing them to an attacker. This is known as secret key distribution.

This document will examine three commonly used classes of cryptographic mechanisms: symmetric algorithms, secure hash algorithms, and asymmetric algorithms. For each class, we will discuss which of the four security services can be supported. In addition, we will discuss whether the algorithm can be used for secret key distribution.

2.3.1 Symmetric Key

Symmetric key cryptography is a class of algorithms where Alice and Bob share a secret key. These algorithms are primarily used to achieve confidentiality, but may also be used for authentication, integrity and limited non-repudiation.

Symmetric algorithms are ideally suited for confidentiality. Modern symmetric algorithms, such as AES, are very fast and very strong. To use a symmetric algorithm for confidentiality, Alice transforms a plaintext message to ciphertext using a symmetric algorithm and a key. Alice transmits the ciphertext to Bob. Bob uses the same key to transform the ciphertext back into the plaintext.

Symmetric algorithms can also be used to authenticate the integrity and origin of data. Alice uses her key to generate ciphertext for the entire plaintext, as above. She sends the plaintext and a portion of the ciphertext to Bob. This portion of the ciphertext is known as a message authentication code, or MAC. Bob uses his copy of the key to generate the ciphertext, selects the same portion of the ciphertext and compares it to the MAC he received. If they match, Bob knows that Alice sent him the message. This does not provide non-repudiation, though. Alice can deny sending the message, since Bob could have generated it himself.

Alice and Bob need to share a symmetric key before Alice encrypts or generates a MAC for a message. Establishing that shared key is called **key management**, and it is a difficult problem. Key management can be performed with symmetric key cryptography, but it is a classic "chicken vs. egg" problem. To use symmetric cryptography, Alice and Bob need to share a secret. Once Alice and Bob share a symmetric encryption key, the algorithm can be used to establish additional shared secrets.

In general, that first shared key must be established through "out-of-band" mechanisms. This is acceptable if Alice communicates only with Bob. If she communicates with a larger community, the burden of establishing each relationship becomes a serious impediment to obtaining security services.

However, this problem can become manageable through the introduction of a trusted third party (TTP). If Alice and the party she wishes to communicate with trust the same TTP, they can get a new key for this purpose from the TTP. Each party must establish a secret out of band with the TTP as a starting point. However, Alice will not need to repeat this process for each new party with which she communicates.

2.3.2   Secure Hash

The secure hash function takes a stream of data and reduces it to a fixed size through a one-way mathematical function. The result is called a message digest and can be thought of as a fingerprint of the data. The message digest can be reproduced by any party with the same stream of data, but it is virtually impossible to create a different stream of data that produces the same message digest.

A message digest can be used to provide integrity. If Alice sends a message and its digest to Bob, he can recompute the message digest to protect against accidental changes in the data. However, this does not protect Bob from an attacker. Charlie can intercept Alice's message and replace it with a new message and the digest of the new message.

A secure hash can be used to create a hash-based message authentication code, or HMAC, if Alice and Bob share a secret key. If Alice sends a message and its HMAC to Bob, he can recompute the HMAC to protect against changes in the data from any source. Charlie can intercept Alice's message and replace it with a new message, but he cannot compute an acceptable HMAC without knowing the secret key. If Bob trusts Alice, he may accept an HMAC as authenticating Alice's identity. However, the services of confidentiality and non-repudiation are not provided. The current Federal standard for a secure hash algorithm is SHA-1, which is specified in FIPS 180-1 [NIST 95]. An Internet Engineering Task Force document, RFC 2104 [IETF 99], describes an open specification for HMAC use on the internet. The RFC 2104 HMAC can be used in combination with any iterated cryptographic hash, such as MD5 and SHA-1. It also provides for use of a secret key to calculate and verify the message authentication values.

2.3.3 Asymmetric (public key) Cryptography

Asymmetric key cryptography, also known as public key cryptography, uses a class of algorithms in which Alice has a private key, and Bob (and others) have her public key. The public and private keys are generated at the same time, and data encrypted with one key can be decrypted with the other key. That is, a party can encrypt a message using Alice's public key, then only Alice, the owner of the matching private key, can decrypt the message. Asymmetric algorithms are poorly suited for encrypting large messages because they are relatively slow. Instead, these algorithms are used to achieve authentication, integrity and non-repudiation, and support confidentiality through key management. Asymmetric algorithms are used to perform three operations explained below: digital signatures, key transport, and key agreement.

Digital Signatures. Alice can generate a digital signature for a message using a message digest and her private key. To authenticate Alice as the sender, Bob generates the message digest as well and uses Alice's public key to validate the signature. If a different private key was used to generate the signature, the validation will fail.

In contrast to handwritten signatures, a digital signature also verifies the integrity of the data. If the data has been changed since the signature was applied, a different digest would be produced. This would result in a different signature. Therefore, if the data does not have integrity, the validation will fail.

In some circumstances, the digital signature can be used to establish non-repudiation. If Bob can demonstrate that only Alice holds the private key, Alice cannot deny generating the signature. In general, Bob will need to rely on a third party to attest that Alice had the private key.

Digital signatures are also used for authentication to systems or applications. A system can authenticate Alice's identity through a challenge-response protocol. The system generates a random challenge and Alice signs it. If the signature is verified with Alice's public key, it must have been signed by Alice. This type of authentication is useful for remote access to information on a server, protecting network management from masqueraders, or for gaining physical access to a restricted area.

Key Transport. Some asymmetric algorithms (e.g., RSA [RSA 78]) can be used to encrypt and decrypt data. In practice these algorithms are never used to encrypt large amounts of data, because they are much slower than symmetric key algorithms. However, these algorithms are perfectly suited to encrypting small amounts of data – such as a symmetric key. This operation is called key transport or key exchange, and is used in many protocols. The following example might describe an electronic mail message from Alice to Bob:

- Alice generates an AES [NIST 01b] key, and encrypts the message. She encrypts the AES key using Bob's public key, and sends both the encrypted key and encrypted message to Bob.
- Bob uses his private key to recover Alice's AES key; he then uses the AES key to obtain the plaintext message.

In this case, Alice uses asymmetric cryptography to achieve confidentiality for key distribution. This procedure does not provide any additional security services; since Alice used Bob's public key, anyone could have generated the message.

Key Agreement. Other asymmetric algorithms (e.g., Diffie-Hellman [DH 76]) may be used for key agreement. Assume Bob and Alice each generated a pair of Diffie-Hellman keys. Alice has her private key and Bob's public key. Bob has his private key and Alice's public key. Through a mathematical algorithm, Alice and Bob both generate the same secret value. Charlie may have both public keys, but he cannot calculate the secret value. Alice and Bob can use the secret value that they independently calculated as the AES key and protect their messages.

There are forms of key agreement that provide implicit authentication as well. If Bob can retrieve the plaintext, he knows it was encrypted by Alice. She is the only one that could have generated the same secret value.

2.3.4   Summary – Cryptographic Mechanisms

Cryptographic mechanisms need to be used in concert to provide a complete suite of security services. Each class of algorithms has strengths and weaknesses.

Symmetric cryptographic algorithms, such as AES, are needed to achieve confidentiality. These algorithms can provide some degree of integrity and authentication as well, but they are poorly suited to achieve non-repudiation. The Achilles heel for symmetric algorithms, however, is key distribution.

The secure hash algorithm and the HMAC provide the basis for data integrity in electronic communications. They do not provide confidentiality, and are a weak tool for authentication or non-repudiation. The secure hash and HMAC cannot be used for key distribution, either.

Symmetric cryptographic algorithms are highly effective for integrity, authentication, and key distribution. Digital signature algorithms, such as RSA or DSA, leverage secure hash algorithms for efficiency. When leveraging a trusted third party, digital signatures can be used to provide non-repudiation. Key transport algorithms (e.g., RSA) and key agreement algorithms (e.g., Diffie-Hellman) can be used to efficiently and securely distribute symmetric keys. Once again, leveraging a trusted third party to establish the identity of the private key holder simplifies the problem.

Many applications will use these three classes of cryptographic mechanisms in concert to achieve the complete suite of security services.

Mechanism		Data integrity	Confidentiality	Identification and authentication	Non-repudiation	Key Distribution
Symmetric key cryptography	Encryption	No	Yes	No	No	No
	Message authentication codes	Yes	No	Yes	No	No
	Key transport	No	No	No	No	Yes-requires out-of-band initialization step or a TTP
Secure Hash Functions	Message digest	Yes	No	No	No	No
	HMAC	Yes	No	Yes	No	No
Asymmetric cryptography	Digital signatures	Yes	No	Yes	Yes (with a TTP)	No
	Key transport	No	No	No	No	Yes
	Key Agreement	No	No	Yes	No	Yes

2.4 SECURITY INFRASTRUCTURES

To achieve the broad range of security services, Alice and Bob will need to use several classes of cryptographic security mechanisms in concert. In particular, to achieve confidentiality they will need to distribute symmetric encryption keys. Distributing symmetric keys can be performed three ways: (1) directly between the parties using symmetric encryption; (2) using symmetric encryption and a trusted third party (TTP); or (3) using public key based key management with a TTP.

The first mechanism is sufficient for small closed communities. If Alice communicates with just three or four people, she can perform an out-of-band initialization with each party. As communities grow, this solution fails to scale, though. What if Alice communicates with dozens of people? Now she needs a TTP to eliminate the out-of-band initialization step. The second mechanism is clearly more scalable, but it provides only limited support for authentication and does not support non-repudiation.

The third mechanism is also scalable, and it also provides a comprehensive solution. If a TTP binds the public key to a user or system – that is, attests to the identity of the party holding the corresponding private key - the complete range of security services may be obtained. The user may obtain integrity, authentication, and non-repudiation through digital signatures. Symmetric keys can be distributed using either key transport or key agreement. Those symmetric keys can be used to achieve confidentiality.

Of course, a single TTP will only scale so far. To achieve security services across organizational boundaries, many inter-linked TTPs will be required. This set of interlinked TTPs forms a security infrastructure that users can rely upon to obtain security services. When this security infrastructure is designed to distribute public keys, it is known as a public key infrastructure (PKI).

3 PUBLIC KEY INFRASTRUCTURES

A public key infrastructure (PKI) binds public keys to entities, enables other entities to verify public key bindings, and provides the services needed for ongoing management of keys in a distributed system.

The overall goals of modern security architectures are to protect and distribute information that is needed in a widely distributed environment, where the users, resources and stake-holders may all be in different places at different times. The emerging approach to address these security needs makes use of the scalable and distributed characteristics of public key infrastructure ("PKI"). PKI allows you to conduct business electronically with the confidence that:

- The person or process identified as sending the transaction is actually the originator.
- The person or process receiving the transaction is the intended recipient.
- Data integrity has not been compromised.

In conventional business transactions, customers and merchants rely on credit cards (e.g., VISA or MasterCard) to complete the financial aspects of transactions. The merchant may authenticate the customer through signature comparison or by checking identification, such as a driver's license. The merchant relies on the information on the credit card and status information obtained from the credit card issuer to ensure that payment will be received. Similarly, the customer performs the transaction knowing they can reject the bill if the merchant fails to provide the goods or services. The credit card issuer is the trusted third party in this type of transaction.

The same model is often applied in electronic commerce, even though the customer and issuer may never meet. The merchant cannot check the signature or request identification information. At best, the merchant can verify the customer's address against the credit card issuer's database. Again, the customer knows that they can reject the bill if the merchant fails to provide the goods or services. The credit card issuer is the trusted third party that makes consumer-to-business e-commerce possible.

With electronic commerce, customer and merchant may be separated by hundreds of miles. Other forms of authentication are needed, and the customer's credit card and financial information must be protected for transmission over the internet. Customers who do business with a merchant over the internet must use encryption methods that enable them to protect the information they transmit to the merchant, and the merchant must protect the information it transmits back to customers. Both customer and merchant must be able to obtain encryption keys and ensure that the other party is legitimate. The PKI provides the mechanisms to accomplish these tasks.

Two parties who wish to transact business securely may be separated geographically, and may not have ever met. To use public key cryptography to achieve their security services, they must be able to obtain each other's public keys and authenticate the other party's identity. This may be performed out-of-band if only two parties need to conduct business. If they will conduct business with a variety of parties, or cannot use out-of-band means, they must rely on a trusted third party to distribute the public keys and authenticate the identity of the party associated with the corresponding key pair.

Public key infrastructure is the combination of software, encryption technologies, and services that enables enterprises to protect the security of their communications and business transactions on networks. PKI integrates digital certificates, public key cryptography, and certification authorities into a complete enterprise-wide network security architecture. A typical enterprise's PKI encompasses the issuance of digital certificates to individual users and servers;

end-user enrollment software; integration with certificate directories; tools for managing, renewing, and revoking certificates; and related services and support.

The term public key infrastructure is derived from public key cryptography, the technology on which PKI is based. Public key cryptography is the technology behind modern digital signature techniques. It has unique features that make it invaluable as a basis for security functions in distributed systems. This section provides additional background on the underlying mechanisms of a public key system.

3.1 PKI COMPONENTS

Functional elements of a public key infrastructure include certification authorities, registration authorities, repositories, and archives. The users of the PKI come in two flavors: certificate holders and relying parties. An attribute authority is an optional component.

A **certification authority (CA)** is similar to a notary. The CA confirms the identities of parties sending and receiving electronic payments or other communications. Authentication is a necessary element of many formal communications between parties, including payment transactions. In most check-cashing transactions, a driver's license with a picture is sufficient authentication. A personal identification number (PIN) provides electronic authentication for transactions at a bank automated teller machine (ATM).

A **registration authority (RA)** is an entity that is trusted by the CA to register or vouch for the identity of users to a CA.

A **repository** is a database of active digital certificates for a CA system. The main business of the repository is to provide data that allows users to confirm the status of digital certificates for individuals and businesses that receive digitally signed messages. These message recipients are called relying parties. CAs post certificates and CRLs to repositories.

An **archive** is a database of information to be used in settling future disputes. The business of the archive is to store and protect sufficient information to determine if a digital signature on an "old" document should be trusted.

The CA issues a **public key certificate** for each identity, confirming that the identity has the appropriate credentials. A digital certificate typically includes the public key, information about the identity of the party holding the corresponding private key, the operational period for the certificate, and the CA's own digital signature. In addition, the certificate may contain other information about the signing party or information about the recommended uses for the public key. A subscriber is an individual or business entity that has contracted with a CA to receive a digital certificate verifying an identity for digitally signing electronic messages.

CAs must also issue and process **certificate revocation lists (CRLs),** which are lists of certificates that have been revoked. The list is usually signed by the same entity that issued the certificates. Certificates may be revoked, for example, if the owner's private key has been lost; the owner leaves the company or agency; or the owner's name changes. CRLs also document the historical revocation status of certificates. That is, a dated signature may be presumed to be valid if the signature date was within the validity period of the certificate, and the current CRL of the issuing CA at that date did not show the certificate to be revoked.

PKI users are organizations or individuals that use the PKI, but do not issue certificates. They rely on the other components of the PKI to obtain certificates, and to verify the certificates of other entities that they do business with. End entities include the *relying party*, who relies on the certificate to know, with certainty, the public key of another entity; and the *certificate holder*, that is issued a certificate and can sign digital documents. Note that an individual or organization may be both a relying party and a certificate holder for various applications.

3.1.1 Certification Authorities

The certification authority, or CA, is the basic building block of the PKI. The CA is a collection of computer hardware, software, and the people who operate it. The CA is known by two attributes: its name and its public key. The CA performs four basic PKI functions: issues certificates (i.e., creates and signs them); maintains certificate status information and issues CRLs; publishes its current (e.g., unexpired) certificates and CRLs, so users can obtain the information they need to implement security services; and maintains archives of status information about the expired certificates that it issued. These requirements may be difficult to satisfy simultaneously. To fulfill these requirements, the CA may delegate certain functions to the other components of the infrastructure.

A CA may issue certificates to users, to other CAs, or both. When a CA issues a certificate, it is asserting that the subject (the entity named in the certificate) has the private key that corresponds to the public key contained in the certificate. If the CA includes additional information in the certificate, the CA is asserting that information corresponds to the subject as well. This additional information might be contact information (e.g., an electronic mail address), or policy information (e.g., the types of applications that can be performed with this public key.) When the subject of the certificate is another CA, the issuer is asserting that the certificates issued by the other CA are trustworthy.

The CA inserts its name in every certificate (and CRL) it generates, and signs them with its private key. Once users establish that they trust a CA (directly, or through a certification path) they can trust certificates issued by that CA. Users can easily identify certificates issued by that CA by comparing its name. To ensure the certificate is genuine, they verify the signature using the CA's public key. As a result, it is important that the CA provide adequate protection for its own private key. Federal government CAs should always use cryptographic modules that have been validated against FIPS 140.

As CA operation is central to the security services provided by a PKI, this topic is explored in additional detail in Section 5, CA System Operation.

3.1.2 Registration Authorities

An RA is designed to verify certificate contents for the CA. Certificate contents may reflect information presented by the entity requesting the certificate, such as a drivers license or recent pay stub. They may also reflect information provided by a third party. For example, the credit limit assigned to a credit card reflects information obtained from credit bureaus. A certificate may reflect data from the company's Human Resources department, or a letter from a designated company official. For example, Bob's certificate could indicate that he has signature authority for small contracts. The RA aggregates these inputs and provides this information to the CA.

Like the CA, the RA is a collection of computer hardware, software, and the person or people who operate it. Unlike a CA, an RA will often be operated by a single person. Each CA will maintain a list of accredited RAs; that is a list of RAs determined to be trustworthy. An RA is known to the CA by a name and a public key. By verifying the RA's signature on a message, the CA can be sure an accredited RA provided the information, and it can be trusted. As a result, it is important that the RA provide adequate protection for its own private key. Federal government RAs should always use cryptographic modules that have been validated against FIPS 140.

3.1.3 PKI Repositories

PKI applications are heavily dependent on an underlying directory service for the distribution of certificates and certificate status information. The directory provides a means of storing and distributing certificates, and managing updates to certificates. Directory servers are typically implementations of the X.500 standard or subset of this standard.

X.500 consists of a series of recommendations and the specification itself references several ISO standards. It was designed for directory services that could work across system, corporate, and international boundaries. A suite of protocols is specified for operations such as chaining, shadowing, and referral for server-to-server communication, and the Directory Access Protocol (DAP) for client to server communication. The Lightweight Directory Access Protocol (LDAP) was later developed as an alternative to DAP. Most directory servers and clients support LDAP, though not all support DAP.

To be useful for the PKI applications, directory servers need to be interoperable; without such interoperability, a relying party will not be able to retrieve the needed certificates and CRLs from remote sites for signature verifications. To promote interoperablility among Federal agency directories and thus PKI deployments, the Federal PKI Technical Working Group is developing a Federal PKI Directory Profile [Chang] to assist agencies interested in participating in the FBCA demonstration effort. It is recommended that agencies refer to this document for the minimum interoperability requirements before standing up their agency directories.

3.1.4 Archives

An archive accepts the responsibility for long term storage of archival information on behalf of the CA. An archive asserts that the information was good at the time it was received, and has not been modified while in the archive. The information provided by the CA to the archive must be sufficient to determine if a certificate was actually issued by the CA as specified in the certificate, and valid at that time. The archive protects that information through technical mechanisms and appropriate procedures while in its care. If a dispute arises at a later date, the information can be used to verify that the private key associated with the certificate was used to sign a document. This permits the verification of signatures on old documents (such as wills) at a later date.

3.1.5 PKI users

PKI Users are organizations or individuals that use the PKI, but do not issue certificates. They rely on the other components of the PKI to obtain certificates, and to verify the certificates of other entities that they do business with. End entities include the relying party, who relies on the certificate to know, with certainty, the public key of another entity; and the certificate holder, that is issued a certificate and can sign digital documents. Note that an individual or organization may be both a relying party and a certificate holder for various applications.

3.2 PKI ARCHITECTURES

Certificate holders will obtain their certificates from different CAs, depending upon the organization or community in which they are a member. A PKI is typically composed of many CAs linked by trust paths. A trust path links a relying party with one or more trusted third parties, such that the relying party can have confidence in the validity of the certificate in use. Recipients of a signed message who have no relationship with the CA that issued the certificate for the sender of the message can still validate the sender's certificate by finding a path between their CA and the one that issued the sender's certificate.

The initial challenge is deploying a PKI that can be used throughout an enterprise (e.g., a company or government agency). There are two traditional PKI architectures to support this goal, **hierarchical** and **mesh** enterprise architectures. More recently, enterprises are seeking to link their own PKIs to those of their business partners. A third approach, **bridge CA** architecture, has been developed to address this problem. These three architectures are described below.

3.2.1 Enterprise PKI Architectures

CAs may be linked in a number of ways. Most enterprises that deploy a PKI will choose either a "mesh" or a "hierarchical" architecture:

- *Hierarchical:* Authorities are arranged hierarchically under a "root" CA that issues certificates to subordinate CAs. These CAs may issue certificates to CAs below them in the hierarchy, or to users. In a hierarchical PKI, every relying party knows the public key of the root CA. Any certificate may be verified by verifying the certification path of certificates from the root CA. Alice verifies Bob's certificate, issued by CA 4, then CA 4's certificate, issued by CA 2, and then CA 2's certificate issued by CA 1, the root, whose public key she knows.

- *Mesh:* Independent CA's cross certify each other (that is issue certificates to each other), resulting in a general mesh of trust relationships between peer CAs. Figure 1 (b) illustrates a mesh of authorities. A relying party knows the public key of a CA "near" himself, generally the one that issued his certificate. The relying party verifies certificate by verifying a certification path of certificates that leads from that trusted CA. CAs cross certify with each other, that is they issue certificates to each other, and combine the two in a **crossCertificatePair**. So, for example, Alice knows the public key of CA 3, while Bob knows the public key of CA 4. There are several certification paths that lead from Bob to Alice. The shortest requires Alice to verify Bob's certificate, issued by CA 4, then CA 4's certificate issued by CA 5 and finally CA 5's certificate, issued by CA 3. CA 3 is Alice's CA and she trusts CA 3 and knows its public key.

Figure 1 illustrates these two basic PKI architectures.

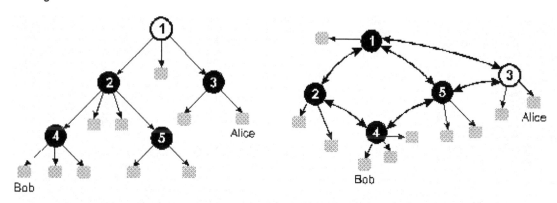

a. hierarchical infrastructure   b. mesh infrastructure

Figure 1. Traditional PKI Architectures

19

3.2.2 Bridge PKI Architecture

The Bridge CA architecture was designed to connect enterprise PKIs regardless of the architecture. This is accomplished by introducing a new CA, called a Bridge CA, whose sole purpose is to establish relationships with enterprise PKIs.

Unlike a mesh CA, the Bridge CA does not issue certificates directly to users. Unlike a root CA in a hierarchy, the Bridge CA is not intended for use as a trust point. All PKI users consider the Bridge CA an intermediary. The Bridge CA establishes peer-to-peer relationships with different enterprise PKIs. These relationships can be combined to form a bridge of trust connecting the users from the different PKIs.

If the trust domain is implemented as a hierarchical PKI, the Bridge CA will establish a relationship with the root CA. If the domain is implemented as a mesh PKI, the bridge will establish a relationship with only one of its CAs. In either case, the CA that enters into a trust relationship with the Bridge is termed a principal CA.

In Figure 2, the Bridge CA has established relationships with three enterprise PKIs. The first is Bob's and Alice's CA, the second is Carol's hierarchical PKI, and the third is Doug's mesh PKI. None of the users trusts the Bridge CA directly. Alice and Bob trust the CA that issued their certificates; they trust the Bridge CA because the Fox CA issued a certificate to it. Carol's trust point is the root CA of her hierarchy; she trusts the Bridge CA because the root CA issued a certificate to it. Doug trusts the CA in the mesh that issued his certificate; he trusts the Bridge CA because there is a valid certification path from the CA that issued him a certificate to the Bridge CA. Alice (or Bob) can use the bridge of trust that exists through the Bridge CA to establish relationships with Carol and Doug.

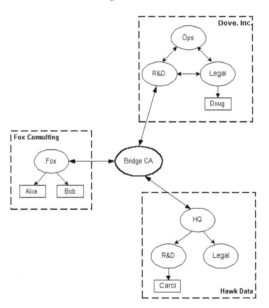

Figure 2. Bridge CA and Enterprise PKIs

3.2.3 Physical Architecture

There are numerous ways in which a PKI can be designed physically. It is highly recommended that the major PKI components be implemented on separate systems, that is, the CA on one system, the RA on a different system, and directory servers on other systems. Because the systems contain sensitive data, they should be located behind an organization's Internet firewall.

The CA system is especially important because a compromise to that system could potentially disrupt the entire operations of the PKI and necessitate starting over with new certificates. Consequently, placing the CA system behind an additional organizational firewall is recommended so that it is protected both from the Internet and from systems in the organization itself. Of course, the organizational firewall would permit communications between the CA and the RA as well as other appropriate systems.

If distinct organizations wish to access certificates from each other, their directories will need to be made available to each other and possibly to other organizations on the Internet. However, some organizations will use the directory server for much more than simply a repository for certificates. The directory server may contain other data considered sensitive to the organization and thus the directory may be too sensitive to be made publicly available. A typical solution would be to create a directory that contains only the public keys or certificates, and to locate this directory at the border of the organization - this directory is referred to as a **border directory**. A likely location for the directory would be outside the organization's firewall or perhaps on a protected DMZ segment of its network so that it is still available to the public but better protected from attack. Figure 3 illustrates a typical arrangement of PKI-related systems.

The main directory server located within the organization's protected network would periodically refresh the border directory with new certificates or updates to the existing certificates. Users within the organization would use the main directory server, whereas other systems and organizations would access only the border directory. When a user in organization A wishes to send encrypted e-mail to a user in organization B, user A would then retrieve user B's certificate from organization B's border directory, and then use the public key in that certificate to encrypt the e-mail.

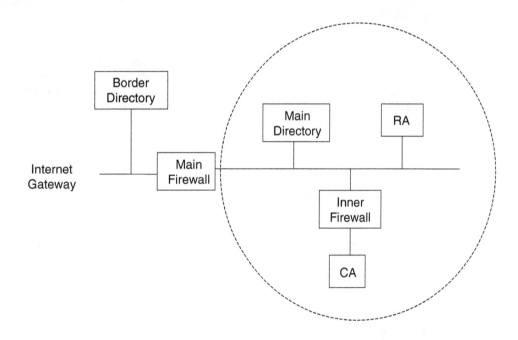

Figure 3. PKI Physical Topology

3.3 PKI DATA STRUCTURES

Two basic data structures are used in PKIs. These are the **public key certificate** and the **certificate revocation lists**. A third data structure, the **attribute certificate**, may be used as an addendum

3.3.1   X.509 Public Key Certificates

The X.509 public key certificate format [IETF 01] has evolved into a flexible and powerful mechanism. It may be used to convey a wide variety of information. Much of that information is optional, and the contents of mandatory fields may vary as well. It is important for PKI implementers to understand the choices they face, and their consequences. Unwise choices may hinder interoperability or prevent support for critical applications.

The X.509 public key certificate is protected by a digital signature of the issuer. Certificate users know the contents have not been tampered with since the signature was generated if the signature can be verified. Certificates contain a set of common fields, and may also include an optional set of extensions.

There are ten common fields: six mandatory and four optional. The mandatory fields are: the serial number, the certificate signature algorithm identifier, the certificate issuer name, the certificate validity period, the public key, and the subject name. The subject is the party that controls the corresponding private key. There are four optional fields: the version number, two unique identifiers, and the extensions. These optional fields appear only in version 2 and 3 certificates.

Version. The version field describes the syntax of the certificate. When the version field is omitted, the certificate is encoded in the original, version 1, syntax. Version 1 certificates do not include the unique identifiers or extensions. When the certificate includes unique identifiers but not extensions, the version field indicates version 2. When the certificate includes extensions, as almost all modern certificates do, the version field indicates version 3.

Serial number. The serial number is an integer assigned by the certificate issuer to each certificate. The serial number must be unique for each certificate generated by a particular issuer. The combination of the issuer name and serial number uniquely identifies any certificate.

Signature. The signature field indicates which digital signature algorithm (e.g., DSA with SHA-1 or RSA with MD5) was used to protect the certificate.

Issuer. The issuer field contains the X.500 distinguished name of the TTP that generated the certificate.

Validity. The validity field indicates the dates on which the certificate becomes valid and the date on which the certificate expires.

Subject. The subject field contains the distinguished name of the holder of the private key corresponding to the public key in this certificate. The subject may be a CA, a RA, or an end entity. End entities can be human users, hardware devices, or anything else that might make use of the private key.

Subject public key information. The subject public key information field contains the subject's public key, optional parameters, and algorithm identifier. The public key in this field, along with the optional algorithm parameters, is used to verify digital signatures or perform key management. If the certificate subject is a CA, then the public key is used to verify the digital signature on a certificate.

Issuer unique ID and **subject unique ID**. These fields contain identifiers, and only appear in version 2 or version 3 certificates. The subject and issuer unique identifiers are intended to handle the reuse of subject names or issuer names over time. However, this mechanism has proven to be an unsatisfactory solution. The Internet Certificate and CRL profile does not [HOUS99] recommend inclusion of these fields.

Extensions. This optional field only appears in version 3 certificates. If present, this field contains one or more certificate extensions. Each extension includes an extension identifier, a criticality flag, and an extension value. Common certificate extensions have been defined by ISO and ANSI to answer questions that are not satisfied by the common fields.

Subject type. This field indicates whether a subject is a CA or an end entity.

Names and identity information. This field aids in resolving questions about a user's identity, e.g., are "alice@gsa.gov" and "c=US; o=U.S. Government; ou=GSA; cn=Alice Adams" the same person?

Key attributes. This field specifies relevant attributes of public keys, e.g., whether it can be used for key transport, or be used to verify a digital signature.

Policy information. This field helps users determine if another user's certificate can be trusted, whether it is appropriate for large transactions, and other conditions that vary with organizational policies.

Certificate extensions allow the CA to include information not supported by the basic certificate content. Any organization may define a private extension to meet its particular business requirements. However, most requirements can be satisfied using standard extensions. Standard extensions are widely supported by commercial products. Standard extensions offer improved interoperability, and they are more cost effective than private extensions.

Extensions have three components: **extension identifier**, a **criticality flag**, and **extension value**. The extension identifier indicates the format and semantics of the extension value. The criticality flag indicates the importance of the extension. When the criticality flag is set, the information is essential to certificate use. Therefore, if an unrecognized critical extension is encountered, the certificate must not be used. Alternatively, an unrecognized non-critical extension may be ignored.

The subject of a certificate could be an end user or another CA. The basic certificate fields do not differentiate between these types of users. The **basic constraints** extension appears in CA certificates, indicating this certificate may be used to build certification paths.

The **key usage** extension indicates the types of security services that this public key can be used to implement. These may be generic services (e.g., non-repudiation or data encryption) or PKI specific services (e.g., verifying signatures on certificates or CRLs).

The subject field contains a directory name, but that may not be the type of name that is used by a particular application. The **subject alternative name** extension is used to provide other name forms for the owner of the private key, such as DNS names or email addresses. For example, the email address alice@gsa.gov.gov could appear in this field.

CAs may have multiple key pairs. The **authority key identifier** extension helps users select the right public key to verify the signature on this certificate.

Users may also have multiple key pairs, or multiple certificates for the same key. The **subject key identifier** extension is used to identify the appropriate public key.

Organizations may support a broad range of applications using PKI. Some certificates may be more trustworthy than others, based on the procedures used to issue them or the type of user cryptographic module. The **certificate policies** extension contains a globally unique identifier that specifies the certificate policy that applies to this certificate.

Different organizations (e.g., different companies or government agencies) will use different certificate policies. Users will not recognize policies from other organizations. The **policy mappings** extension converts policy information from other organizations into locally useful policies. This extension appears only in CA certificates.

The CRL **distribution points** extension contains a pointer to the X.509 CRL where status information for this certificate may be found. (X.509 CRLs are described in the following section.)

When a CA issues a certificate to another CA, it is asserting that the other CA's certificates are trustworthy. Sometimes, the issuer would like to assert that a subset of the certificates should be trusted. There are three basic ways to specify that a subset of certificates should be trusted:

The **basic constraints** extension (described above) has a second role, indicating whether this CA is trusted to issue CA certificates, or just user certificates.

The **name constraints** extension can be used to describe a subset of certificates based on the names in either the subject or subject alternative name fields. This extension can be used to define the set of acceptable names, or the set of unacceptable names. That is, the CA could assert "names in the NIST directory space are acceptable" or "names in the NIST directory space are *not* acceptable."

The **policy constraints** extension can be used to describe a subset of certificates based on the contents of the policy extension. If policy constraints are implemented, users will reject certificates without a policy extension, or where the specified policies are unrecognized.

3.3.2   *Certificate Revocation Lists (CRLs)*

Certificates contain an expiration date. Unfortunately, the data in a certificate may become unreliable before the expiration date arrives. Certificate issuers need a mechanism to provide a status update for the certificates they have issued. One mechanism is the X.509 certification revocation list (CRL).

CRLs are the PKI analog of the credit card hot list that store clerks review before accepting large credit card transactions. The CRL is protected by a digital signature of the CRL issuer. If the signature can be verified, CRL users know the contents have not been tampered with since the signature was generated. CRLs contain a set of common fields, and may also include an optional set of extensions.

The CRL contains the following fields:

Version. The optional version field describes the syntax of the CRL. (In general, the version will be two.)

Signature. The signature field contains the algorithm identifier for the digital signature algorithm used by the CRL issuer to sign the CRL.

Issuer. The issuer field contains the X.500 distinguished name of the CRL issuer.

This update. The this-update field indicates the issue date of this CRL.

Next update. The next-update field indicates the date by which the next CRL will be issued.

Revoked certificates. The revoked certificates structure lists the revoked certificates. The entry for each revoked certificate contains the certificate serial number, time of revocation, and optional CRL entry extensions.

The CRL entry extensions field is used to provide additional information about this particular revoked certificate. This field may only appear if the version is v2.

CRL Extensions. The CRL extensions field is used to provide additional information about the whole CRL. Again, this field may only appear if the version is v2.

ITU-T and ANSI X9 have defined several CRL extensions for X.509 v2 CRLs. They are specified in [X509 97] and [X955]. Each extension in a CRL may be designated as critical or non-critical. A CRL validation fails if an unrecognized critical extension is encountered. However, unrecognized non-critical extensions may be ignored. The X.509 v2 CRL format allows communities to define private extensions to carry information unique to those communities. Communities are encouraged to define non-critical private extensions so that their CRLs can be readily validated by all implementations.

The most commonly used CRL extensions include the following:

The **CRL number** extension is essentially a counter. In general, this extension is provided so that users are informed if an emergency CRL was issued.

As noted in the previous section, CAs may have multiple key pairs. When appearing in a CRL, the **authority key identifier** extension helps users select the right public key to verify the signature on this CRL.

The issuer field contains a directory name, but that may not be the type of name that is used by a particular application. The **issuer alternative name** extension is used to provide other name forms for the owner of the private key, such as DNS names or email addresses. For example, the email address CA1@nist.gov could appear in this field.

The **issuing distribution points** extension is used in conjunction with the CRL distribution points extension in certificates. This extension is used to confirm that this particular CRL is the one described by the CRL distribution points extension and contains status information for certificate in question. This extension is required when the CRL does not cover all certificates issued by a CA, since the CRL may be distributed on an insecure network.

The extensions described above apply to the entire CRL. There are also extensions that apply to a particular revoked certificate.

Certificates may be revoked for a number of different reasons. The user's crypto module may have been stolen, for example, or the module may simply have been broken. The **reason code** extension describes why a particular certificate was revoked. The relying party may use this information to decide if a previously generated signature may be accepted.

Sometimes a CA does not wish to issue its own CRLs. It may delegate this task to another CA. The CA that issues a CRL may include the status of certificates issued by a number of different CAs in the same CRL. The **certificate issuer** extension is used to specify which CA issued a particular certificate, or set of certificates, on a CRL.

3.3.3 Attribute Certificates

The public key certificates described in 3.1.1 are focused on the binding between the subject and the public key. The relationship between the subject and public key is expected to be a long-lived relationship. Most end entity certificates include a validity period of a year or two years.

Organizations seek improved access control. Public key certificates can be used to authenticate the identity of a user, and this identity can be used as an input to access control decision functions. However, in many contexts, the identity is not the criterion used for access control decisions. The access control decision may depend upon role, security clearance, group membership, or ability to pay.

Authorization information, such as membership in a group, often has a shorter lifetime than the binding of the identity and the public key. Authorization information could be placed in a public key certificate extension. However, this is not a good strategy for two reasons. First, the certificate is likely to be revoked because the authorization information needs to be updated. Revoking and reissuing the public key certificate with updated authorization information is quite expensive. Second, the CA that issues public key certificates is not likely to be authoritative for the authorization information. This results in additional steps for the CA to contact the authoritative authorization information source.

The X.509 attribute certificate (AC) binds attributes to an AC **holder** [X509 97]. This definition is being profiled for use in Internet applications. Since the AC does not contain a public key, the AC is used in conjunction with a public key certificate. An access control function may make use of the attributes in an AC, but it is not a replacement for authentication. The public key certificate must first be used to perform authentication, then the AC is used to associate attributes with the authenticated identity.

ACs may also be used in the context of a data origin authentication service and a non-repudiation service. In these contexts, the attributes contained in the AC provide additional information about the signing entity. This information can be used to make sure that the entity is authorized to sign the data. This kind of checking depends either on the context in which the data is exchanged or on the data that has been digitally signed.

An X.509 AC resembles the X.509 public key certificate. The AC is an ASN.1 DER encoded object, and is signed by the issuer. An AC contains nine fields: version, holder, issuer, signature algorithm identifier, serial number, validity period, attributes, issuer unique identifier, and extensions. The AC holder is similar to the public key certificate subject, but the holder may be specified with a name, the issuer and serial number of a public key certificate, or the one-way hash of a certificate or public key. The attributes describe the authorization information associated with the AC holder. The extensions describe additional information about the certificate and how it may be used.

3.4 ADDITIONAL PKI SERVICES

In addition to the security services described previously (non-repudiation, identification and authentication, confidentiality and integrity), PKIs can also offer other services. Two important services that may be offered by a PKI are key recovery and authorization. These services are described below.

Key Recovery. If a user's key is lost, agencies and businesses must still be able to recover data that the employee had encrypted, which can only be done by recovering the encryption key. Reasons for key recovery may include an employee forgetting a password to unlock an encrypted file, the death of an employee who has encrypted some information, or someone attempting to hide criminal activity from law enforcement officials. To ensure the ability to recover encrypted data, encryption keys must be backed up and stored securely.

Note, however, that *signing* keys, i.e., keys used for digital signatures, should not be backed up, since doing so prevents the PKI from ensuring non-repudiation. If anyone other than a particular user has a copy of a signing key, then that user can claim that someone else supplied the signature on a contested document. If a user loses a signing key, a new key and associated certificate can be easily generated. The PKI must keep track of the user's possession of a key, but not the key itself.

Privilege/Authorization. Certificates can be used to vouch for a user's identity and also specify privileges the user has been granted. Privileges might include authority to view classified information or permission to modify material on a Web server among other privileges.

3.5 CASE STUDY

A PKI can support a wide variety of internet and e-commerce applications, including secure electronic mail, virtual private networks, secure web access, and custom applications. The following procurement example illustrates how the services listed above are achieved, and the role played by the major PKI components. For the purposes of this example, we will assume RSA for signatures and key transport, SHA-1 for the hash, and AES for encryption.

Alice is a buyer for the Alpha company. She wishes to obtain widgets from the Beta corporation for Alpha's new product line. The Alpha company does not want its competitors to know anything about the new products – not even that widgets are a subcomponent. Alice wishes to negotiate with Bob, the head of sales at Beta, electronically.

Alice generates two public-private key pairs, one for signature the other for encryption. She goes to the Alpha company RA and provides the signature public key and a valid Alpha company photo-id. The RA verifies the buyer's identity based on the photo-id and vouches for the identity of the buyer to Alpha's CA, who then issues the signature certificate to Alice. The Alpha CA posts the new certificate in the Alpha company directory. Alice returns to her desk and uses her signature to authenticate her request for a key exchange certificate. In this request, Alice provides both her public and private encryption keys. The Alpha CA issues a key transport certificate to Alice and escrows her encryption private key. The Alpha CA also periodically posts a CRL.

The Beta corporation also has a CA. Bob has previously generated his key pairs and obtained certificates. The Beta CA has posted the certificates to its directory. Like the Alpha CA, the Beta CA posts CRLs as well.

Alice constructs a message describing the number of widgets she needs and the schedule for delivery. She signs the message using the private key associated with the public key in her signing certificate. She generates an AES key and encrypts the message. Next, Alice obtains Bob's key transport public key from the Beta directory. Alice verifies that this certificate has not been revoked, and encrypts her AES key using Bob's public key. Alice sends Bob the signed and encrypted message along with the encrypted AES key.

Bob uses his key transport private key to decrypt encrypted AES key. He then uses the AES key to decrypt the message. Now he can read the contents, but is unsure if it really originated from Alice or if it has been changed since Alice created it. Bob obtains Alice's signature certificate from the Alpha directory along with the current CRL. After verifying the certificate has not been revoked, Bob can verify the digital signature on the message. If the signature validates, Bob knows the message came from Alice and has not been modified. He can concentrate on providing an accurate quote to the Alpha company.

Alice and Bob negotiate a deal and the widgets are delivered. The bill arrives, and the Alpha company disputes the cost. This dispute must be settled immediately, or the new product line will be delayed. The CEO needs to see the messages Bob sent to Alice. Unfortunately, Alice is on an adventure vacation and cannot be contacted, so she can not decrypt the messages. The CEO of the Alpha company requests Alice's private encryption key from the escrow server. After determining the request is authentic, the key is returned to the CEO. The CEO uses the key to decrypt the message from the negotiation between Alice and Bob, and the dispute is settled.

We could extend this scenario further to include attribute certificates for authorization. The attribute authority would have issued an attribute certificate to the CEO authorizing him to perform key recovery operations. The escrow server would retrieve and verify the CEO's attribute certificate before approving the escrow request.

4   ISSUES AND RISKS IN CA SYSTEM OPERATION

To issue digital certificates, a CA must verify subscribers' identities; determine the appropriate content of digital certificates; create, distribute, and ensure acceptance of digital certificates; and ensure internal security.   Each of these actions introduces some risk to the parties involved. This section discusses some of these risks and tradeoffs that can be made to reduce or spread the risk[1].

CA systems may be characterized as primarily open or closed. A fully closed system has contracts defining the rights and obligations of all participants for authenticating messages or transactions. This type of system offers the CA operators less risk exposure because there is little uncertainty regarding obligations. Conversely, a fully open system would not have formal contracts defining the rights and obligations of relying parties in the system. In such a system, the firms that perform the CA activities could be exposed to an uncertain level of risk for each authenticated message or transaction. It is likely during early stages of development that most CA systems will be neither fully open nor fully closed, with contracts defining the rights and responsibilities of at least some, but not all, of the system participants.

4.1   VERIFYING IDENTITY

To confirm the identity of a subscriber, the CA either reviews the subscriber's credentials internally or contracts with a registration authority (RA). The decision to outsource and the choice of RA expose the CA to risk. If the CA or RA confirms an identity that is false, or somehow inaccurate, the CA may suffer loss of business or even expose itself to legal actions. Moreover, the CA's outstanding certificates may become suspect if there is a pattern of insufficient due diligence in verifying identities for issuing certificates. The risk exposure from falsely identifying a subscriber may be reduced when a CA issues digital certificates for use within a closed system, because there are contracts in place between some or all of the participants in the system.

4.2   CERTIFICATE CONTENT

Certificates' content varies by CA system. Content and a certificate's limitations are a source of strategic risk to the issuing CA. Standard certificates identify the subscriber and the issuing CA. Another important element of a standard certificate is the expiration date. The X.509 standards for certificate content require that digital certificates contain the distinguished (i.e., unique) name of the certificate issuer (the signer), an issuer-specific serial number, the issuer's signature algorithm identifier, and a validity period. The more limited the life of a certificate, the lower the risk exposure for the issuing CA.   A certificate's security has both physical and logical vulnerabilities that are outgrowths of the software used to generate a digital signature. The longer such software is in use, the greater the likelihood that it will be corrupted or that someone will gain unauthorized access.

Certificate extensions provide information in addition to the identity of the subscriber and the issuing CA. Additional information may include suggested limitations on uses of the certificate, such as the number of and type of transactions or messages that subscribers are authorized to sign. Any such limitation reduces the transaction and reputation risk of the issuing CA. The CA also may use extensions to establish classes of digital certificates for use with financial transactions or for transmitting highly sensitive information. Such certificates may be for a single

---

[1] Portions of this discussion were derived from "Certification Authority Systems", Office of the Comptroller of the Currency, OCC 99-20, May 4, 1999.

message or transaction, used only with a specific relying party, or limited to a maximum financial amount.

4.3 CERTIFICATE CREATION, DISTRIBUTION, AND ACCEPTANCE

The process of creating, distributing, and documenting acceptance of a subscriber's certificate exposes a CA to transaction, strategic, and reputation risk. In certificate creation, the transaction and reputation risk exposures arise from possible errors occurring in the systems that match appropriate certificate limitations to each subscriber's unique signing capabilities. Risk exposures are associated with the policies and procedures that control the process.

Certificate distribution and acceptance often are not solely the responsibility of the CA. The subscriber likely will obtain the technology to create digital signatures from a software provider or other technology firm. However, the certificate is not complete until the CA acknowledges the subscriber's signing capability with its own digital signature to create the certificate of record. In a closed CA system, the CA risk exposure may be modified by the contract establishing the exact roles and responsibilities of the parties. Some of the transaction risk may be allocated to a lead organization, individual subscribers and relying parties, or another entity maintaining the database of certificates. However, the CA still may have a reputation risk exposure if problems with the technology are attributed to the CA.

Generally, a digital certificate will not be operational until the subscriber accepts the signed certificate. Certificate acceptance implies that the subscriber agrees to the terms and conditions established by the CA for the overall system as well as any specific conditions that apply to the subscriber. Errors in the communication process with subscribers regarding acceptance, from either inadequate policies and procedures or technical difficulties, expose the CA to both transaction and reputation risk.

4.4 MANAGING DIGITAL CERTIFICATES

When a CA issues certificates to support subscribers' digital signatures, the CA usually is interacting only with subscribers or a representative or agent acting on behalf of the subscribers. However, if the CA also chooses to manage outstanding certificates, i.e., act as a repository, the CA will transact with relying parties that receive messages. The following discussion outlines the risk exposures that arise with respect to repository services for both subscribers and relying parties. It is organized to address four aspects of managing digital certificates:

- Customer disclosures
- Subscriber service and support;
- Suspending and revoking certificates; and
- Processing the requests of relying parties.

4.4.1 Customer Disclosures

Although there is no legal disclosure requirement at present, a CA will need to provide some information concerning the basic services provided and the rights and responsibilities of subscribers and relying parties. The nature of the disclosures will have an impact both on the transaction and reputation risk exposure of a CA. For example, if disclosures clearly describe the CA error resolution procedures and privacy policy, there may be less confusion on the part of subscribers. Further, if the CA provides technical documentation on the use of the software associated with certificates, subscribers will be better able to distinguish between problems resulting from the software rather than the CA, shifting some of the reputation risk exposure away from the CA.

4.4.2 Subscriber Service and Support

Like many new information technology products and services, a CA requires customer support, which is a source of reputation risk. A CA may consider establishing a help desk or some other form of direct interaction with subscribers and relying parties. The policies, procedures and operation of the help desk are a potential source of transaction and strategic risk. Resolving problems or errors that subscribers and relying parties encounter from lack of familiarity with the use of the underlying technology will require substantial resources from the CA or a customer service contractor. Although the CA typically will not supply software for creating a digital signature, there may be some circumstances in which subscribers attribute all difficulties in using the technology to the CA.

Subscribers may have technical problems because of software configurations on their personal computer systems that may not become apparent until they attempt to sign a message or transaction. Because an organization providing CA services ultimately may wish to maintain the customer relationship, the practical decision may be to provide customer service either internally or to contract with a firm with appropriate expertise. Some technology firms now provide smart cards to hold subscriber certificates. Instead of downloading the software to the PC hard drive, the subscriber would have a smart card reader attached to his PC. The smart card and reader would be pre-programmed to load the certificate information appropriately for the subscriber. Some of the transaction and reputation risk of subscriber service and support may be reduced by the simplicity of the use of hardware rather than requiring PC users to load the software from another source.

4.4.3 Suspending and Revoking Certificates

Because the subscriber is responsible for maintaining the security of the signature capability, the potential exists that the system may be compromised and made available for unauthorized use. Thus, the CA may be required to suspend or revoke a certificate. If the CA (or another responsible party within the system) does not monitor and take such action in a timely manner, the CA may authenticate messages or transactions carrying expired digital signatures. Thus, CA systems that render a subscriber's digital certificate invalid are potentially exposed to substantial transaction, strategic, and reputation risks. Poorly designed policies and procedures are a source of strategic risk, and improperly implemented ones expose the CA to transaction and reputation risk. The timing of necessary repository updates may differ with the type of certificates involved; a delay in the suspension of a certificate used for sensitive messages or transactions carries relatively high risk.

A digital certificate may be rendered invalid in one of two ways. The CA may revoke a certificate if it is certain that a subscriber has compromised his signing capability. The most likely compromise would be if the subscriber did not keep his private key secure. If a subscriber's private key became known, unauthorized individuals could sign messages and transactions. If there is some question as to the status of the certificate, the CA instead may suspend the certificate until its status is determined. Transaction and reputation risk may result from errors in processing both requests for revocation and suspension of certificates. For example, a subscriber whose certificate is erroneously invalidated and hence is unable to sign messages could potentially experience losses and may pursue legal action, damaging the CA's reputation in the process. Conversely, the CA may suffer exposure if a relying party accepts a message or transaction that is signed by a subscriber whose certificate should have been revoked or suspended.

4.4.4 Processing Relying Party Requests

Substantial transaction, strategic, and reputation risk exposure is associated with processing requests by relying parties regarding the status of individual certificates. Although the CA-subscriber contractual relationship may define obligations to subscribers and others, such contracted protection may not exist for transactions with relying parties, particularly in open systems. For example, if the CA represents a revoked certificate as operational to a relying party, the CA may be exposed to reputation damage or a lawsuit. There is an additional risk in an open system that the circumstances of an individual subscriber or class of subscribers have changed during the valid period of a circulating certificate. Any delays in processing certificate revocation requests as a result of inadequate policies and procedures or technical processing may result in such errors. If the repository processes requests in batch mode as opposed to real time, the risk exposure is greater. As the volume of transactions processed by the repository increases and as more certificates are placed in circulation with varying limitations and expiration dates, risk exposures also may increase.

4.4.5 Certificate Revocation

There are two recognized methods for responding to a request about the validity of an individual certificate. The most well known method requires the repository to retrieve a lengthy list of invalid certificates, the Certificate Revocation List (CRL), to check the validity of a single certificate. Inaccuracies in the CRL are a source of transaction risk for the CA system. In addition, the scheduled frequency for generating the CRL will affect the risk exposure of the repository. More frequent generation of CRLs will reduce a CA's transaction and reputation risk exposure. There is also an issue as to whether certificate status is "pushed" out by the CA repository to interested relying parties, or "pulled" from the repository by the relying parties in question.

There are different transaction and reputation risk exposures associated with each method. The "pull" method allows the CA repository to transfer any reputation risk exposure successfully to the relying party with respect to accepting an invalid certificate. On the other hand, the "push" method places the responsibility clearly on the CA if the CRL is not accurate or is not distributed on a timely basis. Because of the risks and cost inefficiencies of the CRL approach, the industry is developing a second method. Several technology firms have developed software that allows a repository to search its records for the validity of a single certificate in real time. Another source of repository transaction risk relates to the ability of a relying party to understand certificate extensions.

5 THE FEDERAL PKI

5.1 FEDERAL PKI ARCHITECTURE

Many Federal agencies have initiated efforts to set up independent CAs to support applications such as purchasing, grants, travel, or other functions that are needed to support the agency mission. For these applications, the use of public key technology must be justified in terms of its direct benefit to a specific agency application. Another option is for the agency to use commercial CA service providers to issue certificates and facilitate delivery of services. Agency projects would then pay the commercial CA service provider.

The main issue for the Federal PKI is how to create certification paths between Federal agencies that will provide for reliable and broad propagation of trust. A Bridge CA (BCA) provides systematic certification paths between CAs in agencies, and outside the government. Federal CAs that meet certain standards and requirements will be eligible to cross-certify with the FBCA, thereby gaining the certification paths needed to establish interoperation between the Federal and commercial PKIs. Figure 4 illustrates how bridge CAs will provide interoperability between Federal and other PKIs.

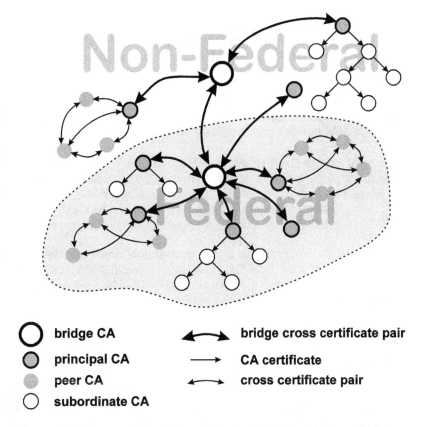

Figure 4. Interoperation Between Federal and Non-Federal PKIs

The Federal BCA will be the unifying element to link otherwise unconnected agency CAs into a systematic overall Federal PKI. It is important to note that the BCA is not a root CA, but is a "bridge of trust". It does not begin certification paths, but connects trust domains through cross certificates between the FBCA and designated principal CAs. A federal policy management authority (FPMA) will supervise FBCA operation and establish the requirements for cross certifying with the FBCA. These trust domains may be within the government or outside the government.

Federal (or non-federal) CAs that operate in trust domains that meet the requirements established by the FPMA will be eligible to cross certify with the FBCA. The FBCA will then connect them to the overall trust network of the Federal PKI. This will provide relying parties and certificate holders (in their trust domains) with connectivity to the larger Federal PKI. This will be simpler and more effective than trying to manage an ad hoc collection of many cross certifications with CAs in other trust domains.

To provide maximum flexibility to Federal agencies and not intrude upon their prerogatives, agencies will not be required to adopt the FBCA's policies. Rather, agencies will retain the option to use other policies defined by their own internal PMAs, or by commercial certificate service providers. Agencies will not be required to use the FBCA to interoperate with other Federal agencies or organizations outside the Federal government. Alternatively, Federal agencies may communicate directly with an agency/organization to establish requirements for interoperating. Components of the Federal PKI architecture are:

Federal Policy Management Authority (FPMA): this management authority sets the overall policies of the Federal PKI and approves the policies and procedures of trust domains within the Federal PKI. It operates a Federal Bridge CA, and a repository.

Trust Domains: In the Federal context, a trust domain is a portion of the Federal PKI that operates under the management of a single policy management authority. One or more CAs exist within each trust domain. Each trust domain has a single principal CA, but may have many other CAs. Each trust domain has a domain repository.

Domain Policy Management Authority (DPMA): a policy management authority approves the certification practice statements of the CAs within a trust domain and monitors their operation. The DPMAs operate or supervise a domain repository.

Federal Bridge CA (FBCA): The Federal Bridge CA is operated by the FPMA. Its purpose is to be a bridge of trust that provides trust paths between the various trust domains of the Federal PKI, as well as between the Federal PKI and non-Federal trust domains. FPMA- approved trust domains designate a principal CA that is eligible to cross-certify with the Federal FBCA. The FBCA is not a root CA because it does not typically begin certification paths.

Principal CA: A CA within a trust domain that cross-certifies with the Federal BCA. Each trust domain has one principal CA. In a domain with hierarchical certification paths, it will be the root CA of the domain. In a mesh-organized domain, the principal CA may be any CA in the domain. However it will typically be one operated by or associated with the DPMA.

Peer CA: A CA in a mesh domain, a peer CA has a self-signed certificate that is distributed to its certificate holders and used by them to initiate certification paths. Peer CAs cross-certify with other CAs in their trust domain.

Root CA: In a hierarchical trust domain, the root CA is the CA that initiates all trust paths. Certificate holders and relying parties are given the self-signed root CA certificate by some authenticated means and all trust paths are initiated from that point. For hierarchical trust domains, the root CA is also the principle CA for that domain.

Subordinate CA: A CA in a hierarchical domain that does not begin trust paths. Trust initiates from some root CA. In a hierarchical trust domain, a subordinate CA receives a certificate from its superior CA. A subordinate CA may have subordinate CAs of its own to which it issues certificates.

5.2 FEDERAL CERTIFICATE PROFILE(S)

In the interest of establishing commonality and interoperability with PKI communities outside the Federal government, it was decided that the FPKI profile should be based on a "standard PKI profile" but still contain the unique parameter settings for Federal systems[2]. The only widely accepted PKI profile currently on track to become a standard is the Internet Engineering Task Force (IETF) Public Key Infrastructure (PKIX) profile (RFC 2459) developed by the PKIX working group. The profile can be found at http://www.ietf.org/rfc/rfc2459. The PKIX profile, Internet X.509 Public Key Infrastructure Certificate and CRL Profile, identifies the format and semantics of certificates and CRLs for the Internet PKI. Procedures are described for processing and validating certification paths in the Internet environment. Encoding rules are provided for cryptographic algorithms and all fields are profiled in both the version 3 X.509 and version 2 CRL.

The FPKI profile complements the current PKIX profile and stipulates any differences between the two. If an organization needs to implement a subset of the FPKI-compliant certificate and/or CRL, the organization should tailor its X.509 certificate and/or CRL using the parameters stipulated in the Federal PKI together with the parameters stipulated in PKIX. Parameters stipulated in the Federal PKI document should take precedence. An organization deciding to tailor its FPKI-compliant X.509 certificate and/or CRLs to meet its specific needs must document the intended subset profile (referencing FPKI profile as a basis) so that the certificate generation element will know how to populate the program-specific certificates [Fed PKI profile].

The federal certificate Profile describes the contents of five classes of X.509 certificates: end entity digital signature certificates; end entity key management certificates; CA certificates, Bridge CA certificates, and self-signed CA certificates.

- End entity digital signature certificates contain a public key that is designated for validation of digital signatures on objects other than certificates and CRLs.
- End entity key management certificates contain a public key that is designated for key transport.
- CA certificates are any certificates issued by an agency CA to another CA.
- Bridge CA certificates are issued by the federal Bridge CA to agency principal CAs.
- Self-signed CA certificates are generated by CAs for secure distribution to their subscribers.

The following table identifies mandatory and optional extensions for each class of certificate. Further details are contained in the profile; agencies should obtain a copy of the current profile, as well as RFC 2459, before deploying their PKI.

---

[2] Portions of this discussion were derived from the Federal Certificate Profile, http://csrc.nist.gov/pki/twg.

Certificate extension	Mandatory or Optional	Contents
Key usage	Appears in all certificates	Specifies the set of generic uses for this key. For users or systems, the key may be used for digital signatures on documents, authentication, key management, or data encipherment. For CAs, the keys may be used for verifying signatures on certificates or CRLs.
Basic constraints	Appears in all CA certificates	Indicates the subject is a CA. May define the maximum number of additional certificates in a path. This is used to limit trust to end entity certificate issued by the subject.
Authority key identifier	Appears in all certificates	SHA-1 hash of the public key which verifies the signature on the certificate; used to select the right key
Subject key identifier	Appears in all CA certificates. May optionally appear in end entity certificates.	SHA-1 hash of this public key; this matches the authority key identifier in certificates and CRLs issued by the subject.
Subject alternative name	Optional, but commonly used.	Used to specify a user's email address, or the DNS name or IP address of an Internet host. This information supports the S/MIME application and IPsec protocols, respectively.
Certificate policies	Appears in all certificates	In an end entity certificate, the policies listed describe the level of trust in this certificate. In a CA certificate, this list describes the range of policies for which its certificates may be trusted.
Policy mapping	Appears only in CA certificates. Appears only when the issuer and subject issue certificates under different policies.	Describes which of the subject CA's policies correspond to the issuer's local policies.
Name constraints	Appears optionally in CA certificates.	Used to limit the set of trusted certificates by name.
Policy constraints	Appears optionally in CA certificates.	Used to impose policy requirements and/or prohibit policy mapping.
CRL distribution points	Optional. Appears in all certificates whose revocation status is distributed by indirect CRLs or segmented CRLs.	Used to identify the CRL that covers this particular certificate.

Certificate extensions in the federal PKI

5.3 FEDERAL CRL PROFILE(S)

The Federal PKI Profile specifies two CRL profiles - one for the FBCA, and a second for all other CAs in the Federal PKI. Both profiles are based on the X.509 Version 2 CRL. The version 2 CRL may include two different types of extensions.

The first type is the CRL entry extension, which provides additional information about a particular revoked certificate. The CRL entry extensions identified in the CRL profiles are the certificate issuer and reason code extensions. By default, all of the certificates listed on a CRL were issued by the CA that generated the CRL. If this is not true, the CRL will use the certificate issuer to identify the CA that issued the certificate. The reason code extension describes the circumstances for revocation. A relying party may accept a certificate that has been "superseded," but reject a certificate that was revoked because of "key compromise."

The second type is the CRL extension, which provides additional information about the entire CRL. The CRL extensions identified by the federal profile are authority key identifier, issuer alternative name, CRL number, and issuing distribution point.

The following tables identify mandatory and optional extensions for each class of CRLs. As noted above, further details are contained in the profile. Agencies should obtain a copy of the current profile, as well as RFC 2459, before deploying their PKI.

CRL Extension	Mandatory or Optional	Contents
CRL number	Appears in all CRLs	Monotonically increasing integer; may be used to detect emergency CRL generation
Authority key identifier	Appears in all CRLs	SHA-1 hash of the public key which verifies the signature on the CRL; used to select the right key
Issuer alternative name	optional	Can be used to specify the CA's email address
Issuing distribution point	Appears in all indirect and segmented CRLs	Contents must match the CRL distribution points extension in the certificates covered by the CRL

CRL Extensions in the Federal PKI

CRL entry extension	Mandatory or Optional	Contents
Reason code	Appears for every certificate, unless the CA has no information	Specifies if the certificate was revoked because the key were compromised, the subject's affiliation changed, or it was superseded by a newer certificate.
Certificate issuer	Appears in all indirect CRLs	Identifies the issuer for a subset of the certificates listed in this CRL.

CRL Entry Extensions in the Federal PKI

6 DEPLOYING AN AGENCY PKI

Agency PKIs will, in most cases, be developed in some degree of isolation. The PKI will be developed to meet internal requirements, where both the subscriber and the relying party are users within that agency. As the agency's confidence and experience increases, it may become cost effective to integrate the agency PKI into the Federal PKI. Adequate planning can ensure that an agency PKI is ready to join the broader Federal PKI, providing access to security services with a growing community of users. This section recommends steps for setting up an agency PKI.

There are numerous impediments and challenges in creating an agency PKI that will interoperate with other federal PKI's. Therefore, it is important to as much as possible follow existing standards and coordinate with the Federal PKI Steering Committee (FPKISC). Some of the challenges an agency will face include the significant cost that can be associated with implementing a PKI, including the cost of creating and distributing certificates, purchasing or creating client software, and in maintaining and supporting users of the PKI. As well, different vendors may implement standards differently, and therefore interoperation of directories and other associated software between PKI's will be tricky.

Accordingly, NIST recommends that agencies follow the steps in this chapter when deploying an agency PKI or PKI pilot. In particular, NIST recommends following the FBCA policy and adhering to the federal certificate profile and CRL extensions profile. It would be best if agencies assume that at some point their PKI will cross-certify with the federal bridge CA, therefore coordinating the development of an agency PKI with the FPKISC is highly recommended. The following sections contain information and steps for developing an agency PKI such that interoperability problems will be minimized.

6.1 ANALYZE DATA AND APPLICATIONS FOR YOUR ORGANIZATION

Installing a PKI can have a significant impact on the security model of an information technology operation. As with most security planning, the agency PKI must be designed using the familiar principles of Risk Management. Planning should begin with risk analysis. In addition to comparing the initial and operating costs of the PKI with anticipated cost-reductions, the cost-benefit analysis should attempt to identify larger risks from not implementing a PKI.

The next step is to identify the data and applications that need to be secured within the agency's computing system. Data may include data used during execution, stored data on magnetic media, printed data, archival data, update logs, audit records, and documentation. Applications may include local/network communications, access controls, and Internet applications. The analysis should also determine the impact if security is compromised, and the degree of risk will determine the appropriate level of assurance for the agency PKI. For example, the more limited the life of a certificate, the lower the risk exposure for the issuing CA. More than one policy may be required if there is a wide variation of risk associated with different applications.

Record retention is always a concern for government agencies, and the movement toward paperless operations will result in significant changes in long-term storage of records. The National Archives and Records Administration (NARA) has developed guidance on records management for agencies implementing electronic signature technologies [NARA00]. The NARA guidance should be consulted during the planning phase to ensure proper record retention practices.

6.2 COLLECT SAMPLE POLICIES AND BASE STANDARDS

It is efficient to begin the development of the PKI by collecting sample policies and using them as templates to develop the agency's own policy(s). Collections of standards are also required for writing your policy(s) because standards are the basis for achieving interoperability between agencies. The following is a list the standards and their references.

> **FBCA policy**   FBCA policy is used for determining which level(s) are consistent with the agency's requirements. Current FBCA policy can be found in http://csrc.nist.gov/pki/twg/y2000/doc_reg_00.htm – Bridge Certification Authorities. Final policy will be posted at http://csrc.nist.gov/csor.

- **FPKI X.509** Certificate and CRL Extensions Profile.   As part of FBCA policy, this document specifies the version 3 (v3) X.509 certificate and version 2 (v2) Certificate Revocation List (CRL) profiles for Federal Public Key Infrastructure (FRKI) systems. The profiles serve to identify unique parameter settings for FPKI. The Federal certificate profile is located at http://csrc.nist.gov/pki/twg/y2000/papers/twg-00-18.xls —Federal Public Key Infrastructure (PKI) X.509 Certificate and CRL Extensions Profile.

- **X.500 directories**   The certificates or other digitally signed instruments issued by the FBCA and, where applicable, agency CAs, will reside in the FBCA X.500 directory. Directory references are listed at http://csrc.nist.gov/pki/twg/directory_references.htm.

6.3 DRAFT CERTIFICATE POLICY(S)

The first requirement for an agency developing a PKI is to establish appropriate certificate policy(s) (CP). The policy(s) must reflect the types of applications that will be secured by the PKI. An effective strategy is to adapt and reuse existing policies (especially FBCA) to create policy(s) for the agency. Certificate policies should be at a sufficiently high level that the policies will not change too frequently. The format and content of these policies is discussed in further detail in section 6.3.1.

The set of policies under which a CA issues certificates is termed its **trust domain** or **policy domain**. The agency needs to obtain an object identifier (OID) for each of the policies in its *trust domain*. These OIDs will be used to differentiate the appropriate set of applications for a particular certificate. An X.509 v3 certificate may state one or more certificate policies in the **certificatePolicy** extension. A **certificatePolicy** extension contains one or more **policyIdentifiers**. A **policyIdentifier** is a unique, registered OID that represents a certificate policy in a certificate. Applications may use these policies to decide whether or not to trust a certificate for a particular purpose. The registration process follows the procedures specified in ISO/IEC, (i.e., joint International Organization for Standardization and International Electrotechnical Commission), and International Telecommunications Union (ITU) standards. The application that registers the OID also needs a textual specification of the certificate policy, for examination by certificate users and other applications. If an agency issues under a single policy, it should still obtain an OID for that policy. When the CA joins the federal PKI, it will be used to differentiate its certificates from the many policies used in the federal government. Procedures to obtain an OID will be covered in section 6.3.2.

6.3.1   Certificate Policies

Policies are generally written in standard format. RFC 2527, the Certificate Policy and Certification Practices Framework, defines the accepted standard CP format. RFC 2527 includes a standard outline with eight major sections and 185 second and third level subsections. Most CPs are written to this outline, since the standard format has a number of distinct advantages. The FBCA CP is consistent with RFC 2527.

By adhering to a well-defined format, the CP writer is less likely to forget something important. It would be easy to overlook a few of the 185 topics identified in RFC 2527 if the author changed the outline. Adhering to the standard format will also simplify cross-certification with other CAs. The cross-certification process should always include a comparison of the other CA's certificate policies. This information is used to determine the contents of the policy mappings and policy constraints extensions to be included in the CA certificates. The eight major sections are summarized below; for details the reader should obtain RFC 2527.

- The **INTRODUCTION** explains how to identify certificates issued under this policy (i.e., the OID that will appear in the policy extension), defines the community for these certificates (e.g., NIST employees, or financial managers,) and provides contact information for the people who administer the CA and maintain the policy.
- The **GENERAL PROVISIONS** captures broadly applicable legal and general practices information. For example, this section identifies the various participants in the PKI (e.g., CA, RAs, subscriber, and relying party) and their various obligations and liabilities. It identifies the applicable laws, fees, and auditing requirements. This section also describes what information (if any) will be considered confidential and the circumstances that would justify disclosure (e.g., a subpoena.).
- **IDENTIFICATION AND AUTHENTICATION** describes the procedures used to authenticate requests for certificates, or for certificate revocation.
- **OPERATIONAL REQUIREMENTS** describes the operations that must be performed by the CA, RAs, end entities, or other parties under this policy. Specific actions are identified that must be performed when requesting or generating new certificates, revoking certificates, creating and protecting audit logs, archiving records, changing the CA's key, disaster recovery, and terminating the CA's operations.
- **PHYSICAL, PROCEDURAL, AND PERSONNEL SECURITY CONTROLS** describes how the PKI uses physical security (e.g., guards, guns, and gates), procedures (e.g., separation of duty), and personnel requirements (e.g., background checks and procedures) to complement the technical security controls.
- **TECHNICAL SECURITY CONTROLS** describes the security measures used to protect cryptographic keys (e.g., a FIPS 140-1 validated hardware module), protect critical security parameters (such as the list of trusted RAs), and provide quality assurance for the systems (e.g., a NIAP evaluation), and protect the CA from network-based attacks.
- **CERTIFICATE AND CRL PROFILES** specifies the certificate and CRL profile. This section specifies the cryptographic algorithms that will be used to sign the certificates, the length of the signing key, and the name forms that will appear in certificates. It describes the extensions that are included in certificates and CRLs. For federal agencies, this should correspond closely to the federal profile discussed above.
- **SPECIFICATION ADMINISTRATION** is the final section, and it describes how the policy will be maintained. It describes the procedures that will be followed if the specification is changed, how those modifications will be published, and the approval procedures.

CP authors should not develop their documents in a vacuum. CP authors should search the available CPs and identify CPs with similar scope and requirements. These CPs should be used as inputs to the CP development process. Example Certificate Policies are available from a number of sources, including U.S. Federal CPs that may be found at http://csrc.nist.gov/csor/pkireg.htm.

6.3.2 Computer Security Objects Registry

As noted above, government agencies should include an appropriate policy OID in all certificates that it issues. NIST maintains the Computer Security Objects Register (CSOR), one of the CSOR's functions is the assignment of object identifiers for PKI certificate policies.

The CSOR has allocated the following registration branch for Public Key Infrastructure (PKI) objects:

csor-certpolicy={joint-iso-ccitt(2) country(16) us(840) organization(1) gov(101) csor(3) pki(2) cert-policy(1)}.

Government agencies may obtain OIDs in this arc by submitting a RFC 2527-formatted Certificate Policy to csor@nist.gov.

In addition, NIST has defined a set of OIDs that may be used during pilot testing of PKIs. The policies associated with these OIDs have no meaning, but may be used to verify the correct operation of certificate policy mechanisms.

6.3.3 Establishing Policy Mappings and Constraints

As agencies progress from a single isolated CA to more sophisticated architectures, they will establish trust relationships between certification authorities. These relationships are manifested as CA certificates. Where CAs issue certificates under common policies, the contents of these certificates are straightforward. The certificate policy extension contains the OIDs for each of the policies shared by the two CAs. There is no need for policy mapping, or policy constraints.

When two CAs issue certificates in different policy domains, procedures become more complicated. Each CA must review the other CA's policies, and determine which of their own policies (if any) they satisfy. These policy relationships are encoded in the policy mapping extensions. If one of the other CA's policies is deemed entirely unacceptable, a CA may include policy constraints in the CA certificate it issues. This extension permits a CA to specify a limited set of policies that are acceptable. As a result, certificates issued under the unacceptable policy will be rejected.

6.3.4 Local certificate and CRL profile(s)

To maximize interoperability, the local certificate and CRL profile must be consistent with the Federal Certificate and CRL Profile described above. That is, the certificate issued by a federal agency must contain all required fields and extensions. The federal agency may mandate inclusion of optional features and add private extensions. However, the private extensions must never be marked as critical. Certificates with unrecognized critical extensions are ignored, so marking private extensions as critical would limit interoperability.

The following table describes consistency:

	Federal Profile	A Consistent Local Profile
Basic certificate fields	Does not use unique identifiers	Does not use unique identifiers
Standard (ISO or IETF) extensions	Mandatory extensions	Mandatory; must match in criticality
	Optional extensions	Mandatory, optional, or never populated. If present must match criticality setting in federal profile.
	Omitted extensions	Must not be used if critical
Private extensions	None	Must be noncritical

6.4 SELECT PKI PRODUCT OR SERVICE PROVIDER

The next step after planning is to select the appropriate PKI product or service provider. The agency needs to review the candidate products or service providers to determine which can implement the agency's policy(s). The following lists aspects to be considered for the selection.

- Compatibility and interoperability with other PKI products/service providers.
- Ease of adoption to open standards.
- Minimum proprietary application program interface (API) dependency.
- Ease of supporting applications such as virtual private networks, access control, secure e-commerce, smartcard management, smartcards and hardware, directories, secure messaging, secure forms, enterprise, and others.
- Ease of deployment.
- Flexibility of administration.
- Scalability and portability of installation.

6.5 DEVELOP CPS (CERTIFICATION PRACTICE STATEMENT)

After the selection of vendor product or service provider the agency need to develop a highly specific document, a CPS (Certification Practice Statements), that describes how an agency (or service provider) will implement the policy(s) developed in 6.3. A CPS is a statement of the practices that a particular CA employs in issuing certificates. A CPS describes the details of the system used and the practices employed by a CA to issue certificates, and it details the procedures used to implement the policies identified in the certificates issued by a CA, including the means used to identify certificate subjects. The CPS also states the means used to protect the private key of the CA, and the other operational practices followed by the CA to ensure security. Each Federal CA will post its CPS in the BCA Repository, and also post the CPS in any repository associated with the CA. The basic list of topics to be covered is the same for both a certificate policy (CP) and a CPS as stated in Section 6.3.1.

6.6 Do a Pilot

PKIs are non-trivial. It is recommended that the agency start by supporting a limited number of users and use it for internal applications first. During the pilot the following operations need to be exercised:

- Set up test accounts (users) for all application that will use the PKI.
- Test all the administration operations to make sure they all work properly.
- Shut down the system, bring it back up, and check that everything works correctly.
- Test all PKI functions of the applications locally and remotely (through network if applicable).
- Make sure that the agency has the physical security and personnel controls in place to support the PKI.
- Repeat 6.3, 6.4, and 6.5 to incorporate lessons learned.

6.7 Apply for Cross Certification with the FBCA

Once the PKI and critical applications work well internally the agency may choose to cross-certify directly with the agencies it commonly deals with. However, the most efficient mechanism for joining the federal PKI is cross-certification with the FBCA. To join the FBCA, one of the important steps is to establish policy mappings and constraints as described in 6.3.1

If the agency wishes to cross-certify its PKI with the FBCA, the first step is to select a principal CA. If the agency PKI has only one CA, it is the principal CA. If the agency PKI is a hierarchy, the principal CA must be the root CA. If the agency PKI is a mesh, the agency is free to select any of its CAs as the principal CA.

The FBCA Policy Management Authority processes requests to cross-certify with the bridge. While procedures are still being finalized, the FBCA will require an agency to submit its CP(s) and may request an independent audit to ensure the CP is being implemented faithfully. The FBCA will determine a mapping between its four certificate policies, which specify four increasing levels of assurance, and the policies that comprise the agency PKI's trust domain. Once an agency PKI cross-certifies with the FBCA, that agency is given a seat in the FBCA Policy Authority.

7 SUMMARY AND CONCLUSIONS

As Federal agency operations are moved online, information technology security services based on cryptography become essential. Public key cryptography can play an important role in providing needed security services including confidentiality, integrity, authentication, and digital signatures. Public key cryptography uses two electronic keys: a public key and a private key. The public key can be known by anyone while the private key is kept secret by its owner.

Public key cryptography is straightforward to implement for a pair of users and a single application. This technology will scale easily to support a few applications or a small community of users. However, as the community grows, it becomes difficult to distribute the public keys and keep track of the user that owns the corresponding private key. To use public key cryptography on a broad scale, users need the support of a security infrastructure to manage public keys.

A public key infrastructure (PKI) allows public key cryptography to be employed on a broad scale. With a PKI, parties who have not met in person are able to engage in verifiable transactions. The identity of the originator of a message can be traced to the owner of the private key as long as there is strong binding between the owner and the owner's public key. A PKI provides the means to bind public keys to their owners and helps in the reliable distribution of public keys in large heterogeneous networks. Public keys are bound to their owners by public key certificates. These certificates contain information such as the owner's name and the associated public key and are issued by a reliable Certification Authority (CA).

A PKI is often composed of many CAs linked by trust paths. The CAs may be linked in several ways. They may be arranged hierarchically under a "root CA" that issues certificates to subordinate CAs. The CAs can also be arranged independently in a network. Recipients of a signed message with no relationship with the CA that issued the certificate for the sender of the message can still validate the sender's certificate by finding a path between their CA and the one that issued the sender's certificate.

The confidence that can be placed on the binding between a public key and its owner depends much on the confidence that can be placed on the CA that issued the certificate that binds them. Provisions in the X.509 standard enable the identification of policies that indicate the strength of mechanisms used and the do's and don'ts of certificate handling. The rules expressed by certificate policies are reflected in certification practice statements (CPSs) that detail the operational rules and system features of CAs and other PKI components. By examining the policies associated with a sender's certificate, the recipient of a signed or encrypted message can determine whether the binding between the sender and the sender's key is acceptable and thus accept or reject the message. By examining a CA's CPS, users can determine whether to obtain certificates from it, based on their security requirements. Other CAs can also use the CPS to determine if they want to cross-certify with that CA.

This publication may be used to assist Federal agency decision-makers in determining if a PKI is needed by their agency, and how PKI services can be deployed most effectively within an agency. It provides an overview of PKI functions and their applications. Additional documentation will be required to fully analyze the costs and benefits of PKI systems for agency use, and to develop plans for their implementation. This document provides a starting point and references to more comprehensive publications.

8 ACRONYMS AND ABBREVIATIONS

ACES	Access Certificates for Electronic Services
API	Application programming interface
ARL	Authority Revocation List
CA	Certification Authority
CP	Certificate Policy
CPS	Certification Practice Statement
CRL	Certificate Revocation List
CSOR	Computer Security Object Registry
DN	Distinguished Name
DSA	Digital Signature Algorithm
DSS	Digital Signature Standard
ECA	External certification authority
ERC	Enhanced Reliability Check
FAR	Federal Acquisition Regulations
FBCA	Federal Bridge Certification Authority
FBCA OA	Federal Bridge Certification Authority Operational Authority
FED-STD	Federal Standard
FIPS PUB	Federal Information Processing Standard Publication
FPKISC	Federal PKI Steering Committee
FPKIPA	Federal PKI Policy Authority
GITSB	Government Information Technology Services Board
GPEA	Government Paperwork Elimination Act of 1998
IETF	Internet Engineering Task Force
ISO	International Organization for Standardization
ITU	International Telecommunications Union
ITU-T	International Telecommunications Union – Telecommunications Sector
ITU-TSS	International Telecommunications Union – Telecommunications System Sector
MOA	Memorandum of Agreement (as used in the context of this CP, between an Agency and the FPKIPA allowing interoperation between the FBCA and Agency Principal CA)
NIST	National Institute of Standards and Technology
NSA	National Security Agency
OID	Object Identifier
PIN	Personal Identification Number
PKI	Public Key Infrastructure
PKIX	Public Key Infrastructure X.509
RA	Registration Authority
RFC	Request For Comments
RSA	Rivest-Shamir-Adleman
SHA-1	Secure Hash Algorithm, Version 1
SSL	Secure Sockets Layer
URL	Uniform Resource Locator
U.S.C.	United States Code
WWW	World Wide Web

9 GLOSSARY

Access	Ability to make use of any information system (IS) resource.
Access Control	Process of granting access to information system resources only to authorized users, programs, processes, or other systems.
Accreditation	Formal declaration by a Designated Approving Authority that an Information System is approved to operate in a particular security mode using a prescribed set of safeguards at an acceptable level of risk.
Activation Data	Private data, other than keys, that are required to access cryptographic modules (i.e., unlock private keys for signing or decryption events).
Agency	Any department, subordinate element of a department, or independent organizational entity that is statutorily or constitutionally recognized as being part of the Executive Branch of the Federal Government.
Agency CA	A CA that acts on behalf of an Agency, and is under the operational control of an Agency.
Applicant	The subscriber is sometimes also called an "applicant" after applying to a certification authority for a certificate, but before the certificate issuance procedure is completed.
Archive	Long-term, physically separate storage.
Attribute Authority	An entity, recognized by the Federal PKI Policy Authority or comparable Agency body as having the authority to verify the association of attributes to an identity.
Audit	Independent review and examination of records and activities to assess the adequacy of system controls, to ensure compliance with established policies and operational procedures, and to recommend necessary changes in controls, policies, or procedures. [NS4009]
Audit Data	Chronological record of system activities to enable the reconstruction and examination of the sequence of events and changes in an event. [NS4009, "audit trail"]
Authenticate	To confirm the identity of an entity when that identity is presented.
Authentication	Security measure designed to establish the validity of a transmission, message, or originator, or a means of verifying an individual's authorization to receive specific categories of information. [NS4009]
Backup	Copy of files and programs made to facilitate recovery if necessary. [NS4009]
Binding	Process of associating two related elements of information. [NS4009]
Biometric	A physical or behavioral characteristic of a human being.
Certificate	A digital representation of information which at least (1) identifies the certification authority issuing it, (2) names or identifies its subscriber, (3) contains the subscriber's public key, (4) identifies its operational period, and (5) is digitally signed by the certification authority issuing it. [ABADSG]. As used in this CP, the term "Certificate" refers to certificates that expressly reference the OID of this CP in the "Certificate Policies" field of an X.509 v.3 certificate.

Certification Authority (CA)	An authority trusted by one or more users to issue and manage X.509 Public Key Certificates and CARLs or CRLs.
Certification Authority Revocation List (CARL)	A signed, time-stamped list of serial numbers of CA public key certificates, including cross-certificates, that have been revoked.
CA Facility	The collection of equipment, personnel, procedures and structures that are used by a Certification Authority to perform certificate issuance and revocation.
Certificate	A digital representation of information which at least (1) identifies the certification authority issuing it, (2) names or identifies it's Subscriber, (3) contains the Subscriber's public key, (4) identifies it's operational period, and (5) is digitally signed by the certification authority issuing it. [ABADSG]
Certificate Management Authority (CMA)	A Certification Authority or a Registration Authority.
Certification Authority Software	Key Management and cryptographic software used to manage certificates issued to subscribers.
Certificate Policy (CP)	A Certificate Policy is a specialized form of administrative policy tuned to electronic transactions performed during certificate management. A Certificate Policy addresses all aspects associated with the generation, production, distribution, accounting, compromise recovery and administration of digital certificates. Indirectly, a certificate policy can also govern the transactions conducted using a communications system protected by a certificate-based security system. By controlling critical certificate extensions, such policies and associated enforcement technology can support provision of the security services required by particular applications.
Certification Practice Statement (CPS)	A statement of the practices that a CA employs in issuing, suspending, revoking and renewing certificates and providing access to them, in accordance with specific requirements (i.e., requirements specified in this CP, or requirements specified in a contract for services).
Certificate-Related Information	Information, such as a subscriber's postal address, that is not included in a certificate. May be used by a CA managing certificates.
Certificate Revocation List (CRL)	A list maintained by a Certification Authority of the certificates which it has issued that are revoked prior to their stated expiration date.
Certificate Status Authority	A trusted entity that provides on-line verification to a Relying Party of a subject certificate's trustworthiness, and may also provide additional attribute information for the subject certificate.
Client (application)	A system entity, usually a computer process acting on behalf of a human user, that makes use of a service provided by a server.
Common Criteria	A set of internationally accepted semantic tools and constructs for describing the security needs of customers and the security attributes of products.

Compromise	Disclosure of information to unauthorized persons, or a violation of the security policy of a system in which unauthorized intentional or unintentional disclosure, modification, destruction, or loss of an object may have occurred.
Computer Security Objects Registry (CSOR)	Computer Security Objects Registry operated by the National Institute of Standards and Technology.
Confidentiality	Assurance that information is not disclosed to unauthorized entities or processes. [NS4009]
Cross-Certificate	A certificate used to establish a trust relationship between two Certification Authorities.
Cryptographic Module	The set of hardware, software, firmware, or some combination thereof that implements cryptographic logic or processes, including cryptographic algorithms, and is contained within the cryptographic boundary of the module. [FIPS1401]
Cryptoperiod	Time span during which each key setting remains in effect.
Data Integrity	Assurance that the data are unchanged from creation to reception.
Digital Signature	The result of a transformation of a message by means of a cryptographic system using keys such that a Relying Party can determine: (1) whether the transformation was created using the private key that corresponds to the public key in the signer's digital certificate; and (2) whether the message has been altered since the transformation was made.
Dual Use Certificate	A certificate that is intended for use with both digital signature and data encryption services.
Duration	A field within a certificate that is composed of two subfields; "date of issue" and "date of next issue".
E-commerce	The use of network technology (especially the internet) to buy or sell goods and services.
Employee	Any person employed by an Agency as defined above.
Encrypted Network	A network on which messages are encrypted (e.g. using DES, AES, or other appropriate algorithms) to prevent reading by unauthorized parties.
Encryption Certificate	A certificate containing a public key that is used to encrypt electronic messages, files, documents, or data transmissions, or to establish or exchange a session key for these same purposes.
End Entity	Relying Parties and Subscribers.
Federal Bridge Certification Authority (FBCA)	The Federal Bridge Certification Authority consists of a collection of Public Key Infrastructure components (Certificate Authorities, Directories, Certificate Policies and Certificate Practice Statements) that are used to provide peer to peer interoperability among Agency Principal Certification Authorities.
Federal Bridge Certification Authority Membrane	The Federal Bridge Certification Authority Membrane consists of a collection of Public Key Infrastructure components including a variety of Certification Authority PKI products, Databases, CA specific Directories, Border Directory, Firewalls, Routers, Randomizers, etc.

FBCA Operational Authority	The Federal Bridge Certification Authority Operational Authority is the organization selected by the Federal Public Key Infrastructure Policy Authority to be responsible for operating the Federal Bridge Certification Authority.
Federal Public Key Infrastructure Policy Authority (FPKI PA)	The Federal PKI Policy Authority is a federal government body responsible for setting, implementing, and administering policy decisions regarding interagency PKI interoperability that uses the FBCA.
Firewall	Gateway that limits access between networks in accordance with local security policy. [NS4009]
High Assurance Guard (HAG)	An enclave boundary protection device that controls access between a local area network that an enterprise system has a requirement to protect, and an external network that is outside the control of the enterprise system, with a high degree of assurance.
Information System Security Officer (ISSO)	Person responsible to the designated approving authority for ensuring the security of an information system throughout its lifecycle, from design through disposal. [NS4009]
Inside threat	An entity with authorized access that has the potential to harm an information system through destruction, disclosure, modification of data, and/or denial of service.
Integrity	Protection against unauthorized modification or destruction of information. [NS4009]. A state in which information has remained unaltered from the point it was produced by a source, during transmission, storage, and eventual receipt by the destination.
Intellectual Property	Useful artistic, technical, and/or industrial information, knowledge or ideas that convey ownership and control of tangible or virtual usage and/or representation.
Intermediate CA	A CA that is subordinate to another CA, and has a CA subordinate to itself.
Key Escrow	A deposit of the private key of a subscriber and other pertinent information pursuant to an escrow agreement or similar contract binding upon the subscriber, the terms of which require one or more agents to hold the subscriber's private key for the benefit of the subscriber, an employer, or other party, upon provisions set forth in the agreement. [adapted from ABADSG, "Commercial key escrow service"]
Key Exchange	The process of exchanging public keys in order to establish secure communications.
Key Generation Material	Random numbers, pseudo-random numbers, and cryptographic parameters used in generating cryptographic keys.
Key Pair	Two mathematically related keys having the properties that (1) one key can be used to encrypt a message that can only be decrypted using the other key, and (ii) even knowing one key, it is computationally infeasible to discover the other key.
Local Registration Authority (LRA)	A Registration Authority with responsibility for a local community.
Memorandum	Agreement between the Federal PKI Policy Authority and an Agency allowing

of Agreement (MOA)	interoperability between the Agency Principal CA and the FBCA.
Mission Support Information	Information that is important to the support of deployed and contingency forces.
Mutual Authentication	Occurs when parties at both ends of a communication activity authenticate each other (see authentication).
Naming Authority	An organizational entity responsible for assigning distinguished names (DNs) and for assuring that each DN is meaningful and unique within its domain.
Non-Repudiation	Assurance that the sender is provided with proof of delivery and that the recipient is provided with proof of the sender's identity so that neither can later deny having processed the data. [NS4009] Technical non-repudiation refers to the assurance a Relying Party has that if a public key is used to validate a digital signature, that signature had to have been made by the corresponding private signature key. Legal non-repudiation refers to how well possession or control of the private signature key can be established.
Object Identifier (OID)	A specialized formatted number that is registered with an internationally recognized standards organization. The unique alphanumeric/numeric identifier registered under the ISO registration standard to reference a specific object or object class. In the federal government PKI they are used to uniquely identify each of the four policies and cryptographic algorithms supported.
Out-of-Band	Communication between parties utilizing a means or method that differs from the current method of communication (e.g., one party uses U.S. Postal Service mail to communicate with another party where current communication is occurring online).
Outside Threat	An unauthorized entity from outside the domain perimeter that has the potential to harm an Information System through destruction, disclosure, modification of data, and/or denial of service.
Physically Isolated Network	A network that is not connected to entities or systems outside a physically controlled space.
PKI Sponsor	Fills the role of a Subscriber for non-human system components that are named as public key certificate subjects, and is responsible for meeting the obligations of Subscribers as defined throughout this CP.
Policy Management Authority (PMA)	Body established to oversee the creation and update of Certificate Policies, review Certification Practice Statements, review the results of CA audits for policy compliance, evaluate non-domain policies for acceptance within the domain, and generally oversee and manage the PKI certificate policies. For the FBCA, the PMA is the Federal PKI Policy Authority.
Principal CA	The Principal CA is a CA designated by an Agency to interoperate with the FBCA. An Agency may designate multiple Principal CAs to interoperate with the FBCA.
Privacy	Restricting access to subscriber or Relying Party information in accordance with Federal law and Agency policy.
Private Key	(1) The key of a signature key pair used to create a digital signature. (2) The key of an encryption key pair that is used to decrypt confidential information. In both cases, this key must be kept secret.
Public Key	(1) The key of a signature key pair used to validate a digital signature. (2) The key of

	an encryption key pair that is used to encrypt confidential information. In both cases, this key is made publicly available normally in the form of a digital certificate.
Public Key Infrastructure (PKI)	A set of policies, processes, server platforms, software and workstations used for the purpose of administering certificates and public-private key pairs, including the ability to issue, maintain, and revoke public key certificates.
Registration Authority (RA)	An entity that is responsible for identification and authentication of certificate subjects, but that does not sign or issue certificates (i.e., a Registration Authority is delegated certain tasks on behalf of an authorized CA).
Re-key (a certificate)	To change the value of a cryptographic key that is being used in a cryptographic system application; this normally entails issuing a new certificate on the new public key.
Relying Party	A person or Agency who has received information that includes a certificate and a digital signature verifiable with reference to a public key listed in the certificate, and is in a position to rely on them.
Renew (a certificate)	The act or process of extending the validity of the data binding asserted by a public key certificate by issuing a new certificate.
Repository	A database containing information and data relating to certificates as specified in this CP; may also be referred to as a directory.
Responsible Individual	A trustworthy person designated by a sponsoring organization to authenticate individual applicants seeking certificates on the basis of their affiliation with the sponsor.
Revoke a Certificate	To prematurely end the operational period of a certificate effective at a specific date and time.
Risk	An expectation of loss expressed as the probability that a particular threat will exploit a particular vulnerability with a particular harmful result.
Risk Tolerance	The level of risk an entity is willing to assume in order to achieve a potential desired result.
Root CA	In a hierarchical PKI, the CA whose public key serves as the most trusted datum (i.e., the beginning of trust paths) for a security domain.
Server	A system entity that provides a service in response to requests from clients.
Signature Certificate	A public key certificate that contains a public key intended for verifying digital signatures rather than encrypting data or performing any other cryptographic functions.
Subordinate CA	In a hierarchical PKI, a CA whose certificate signature key is certified by another CA, and whose activities are constrained by that other CA. (See superior CA).
Subscriber	A Subscriber is an entity that (1) is the subject named or identified in a certificate issued to that entity, (2) holds a private key that corresponds to the public key listed in the certificate, and (3) does not itself issue certificates to another party. This includes, but is not limited to, an individual or network device
Superior CA	In a hierarchical PKI, a CA who has certified the certificate signature key of another CA, and who constrains the activities of that CA. (See subordinate CA).
System Equipment	A comprehensive accounting of all system hardware and software types and settings.

Configuration	
Technical non-repudiation	The contribution public key mechanisms to the provision of technical evidence supporting a non-repudiation security service.
Threat	Any circumstance or event with the potential to cause harm to an information system in the form of destruction, disclosure, adverse modification of data, and/or denial of service. [NS4009]
Trust List	Collection of trusted certificates used by Relying Parties to authenticate other certificates.
Trusted Agent	Entity authorized to act as a representative of an Agency in confirming Subscriber identification during the registration process. Trusted Agents do not have automated interfaces with Certification Authorities.
Trusted Certificate	A certificate that is trusted by the Relying Party on the basis of secure and authenticated delivery. The public keys included in trusted certificates are used to start certification paths. Also known as a "trust anchor".
Trusted Timestamp	A digitally signed assertion by a trusted authority that a specific digital object existed at a particular time.
Trustworthy System	Computer hardware, software and procedures that: (1) are reasonably secure from intrusion and misuse; (2) provide a reasonable level of availability, reliability, and correct operation; (3) are reasonably suited to performing their intended functions; and (4) adhere to generally accepted security procedures.
Update (a certificate)	The act or process by which data items bound in an existing public key certificate, especially authorizations granted to the subject, are changed by issuing a new certificate.

10 SELECTED BIBLIOGRAPHY

[BDNP 98] Burr, W., D. Dodson, N. Nazario, W.T. Polk. *Minimum Interoperability Specification for PKI Components (MISPC), Version 1.* NIST SP 800-15. National Institute of Standards and Technology, January 1998.
http://csrc.nist.gov/publications/nistpubs/800-15/SP800-15.PDF

[CJB 01] Chang, S., Johnson, R., and W. Burr, "Federal PKI Directory Profile", working document, http://csrc.nist.gov/pki/twg/y2001/doc_reg_01.htm.

[COOP 99] Cooper, D.A. "A model of certificate revocation," Proceedings of the Fifteenth Annual Computer Security Applications Conference, pages 256-264, December 1999.

[DH 76] W. Diffie, M.E. Hellman, "New Directions in Cryptography," IEEE Transactions on Information Theory, v. IT-22, n. 6, (Nov 1976), pp. 644-654.

[ENTR 00] Entrust Technologies. "The PKI: Paving the Way for Secure Electronic Service Delivery," January, 2000.

[HCFA 01] The Health Insurance Portability and Accountability Act of 1996 (HIPAA) Page, http://www.hcfa.gov/hipaa/hipaahm.htm

[HP 01] Housley, R., and W.T. Polk. *Planning for PKI: Best practices for PKI Deployment,* Wiley & Sons, 2001.

[IETF 99] RFC 2104 HMAC: Keyed-Hashing for Message Authentication.
http://www.ietf.org/rfc/rfc2104.txt

[IETF 01] Public-Key Infrastructure (X.509) (pkix)
http://www.ietf.org/html.charters/pkix-charter.html

[LEE 99] Lee, A. *Guideline for Implementing Cryptography in the Federal Government,* NIST SP 800-21. National Institute of Standards and Technology, November, 1999.
http://csrc.nist.gov/publications/nistpubs/800-21/800-21.pdf

[LYON 00] Lyons-Burke, K. "Federal Agency Use of Public Key Technology for Digital Signatures and Authentication," NIST Special Publication 800-25, October 2000.
http://csrc.nist.gov/publications/nistpubs/800-12/

[MOSE 99] Moses, T. "Trust Management in the Public Key Infrastructure," Entrust Technologies, January 14, 1999. http://www.entrust.com/resources/pdf/trustmodels.pdf

[NARA 00] National Archives and Records Administration, "Records Management Guidance for Agencies Implementing Electronic Signature Technologies", October 18, 2000", http://www.nara.gov/records/policy/gpea.html

[NIST 01] National Institute of Standards and Technology. *Certificate Issuing and Management Components Protection Profile,*
http://csrc.nist.gov/pki/documents/CIMC_PP_final-corrections_20010126.pdf

[NIST 97] National Institute of Standards and Technology. Public Key Infrastructure Technology, ITL Bulletin, July 1997. http://www.nist.gov/itl/lab/bulletns/archives/july97bull.htm

[NIST 94] National Institute of Standards and Technology. FIPS 140-1, *Security Requirements for Cryptographic Modules,* Jan. 1994.
http://csrc.nist.gov/publications/fips/fips1401.htm

[NIST 95] National Institute of Standards and Technology. FIPS 180-1, *Secure Hash Standard*, April 1995. http://csrc.nist.gov/publications/fips/fips180-1/fip180-1.pdf

[NIST 00] National Institute of Standards and Technology. "X.509 Certificate Policy for the Federal Bridge Certification Authority (FBCA), Version 1.4R, March 4, 2000. http://csrc.nist.gov/pki/fbca/FBCA_CP_20001227.doc

[NIST 01b] "Draft FIPS for the AES", http://csrc.nist.gov/encryption/aes/index.html.

[RSA 78] R.L. Rivest, A. Shamir, L.M. Adleman, "A Method for Obtaining Digital Signatures and Public-Key Cryptosystems," Communications of the ACM, v. 21, n. 2 (Feb 1978), pp. 120-126.

[TREA 99] Office of the Comptroller of the Currency. "Certification Authority Systems", OCC 99-20, May 4, 1999.

www.ingramcontent.com/pod-product-compliance
Lightning Source LLC
Chambersburg PA
CBHW061628080326
40690CB00058B/4301